Ladies on Horseback, by Nannie Lambert

Title: Ladies on Horseback Learning, Park-Riding, and Hunting, with Hints upon Costume, and Numerous Anecdotes

Author: Nannie Lambert

Release Date: April 21, 2012 [EBook #39501]

Language: English

Character set encoding: ISO-8859-1

[Illustration: A woman dressed in riding clothes]

LADIES ON HORSEBACK.

LEARNING, PARK-RIDING, AND HUNTING, WITH HINTS UPON COSTUME, AND NUMEROUS ANECDOTES.

BY

MRS. POWER O'DONOGHUE (NANNIE LAMBERT).

AUTHORESS OF "THE KNAVE OF CLUBS," "HORSES AND HORSEMEN," "GRANDFATHER'S HUNTER," "ONE IN TEN THOUSAND," "SPRING LEAVES," "THOUGHTS ON THE TALMUD," ETC., ETC.

LONDON: W. H. ALLEN & CO., 13, WATERLOO PLACE, S.W.

1881.

LONDON: PRINTED BY W. H. ALLEN AND CO., 13, WATERLOO PLACE, S.W.

TO MY FRIEND ALFRED E. T. WATSON, ESQ., AUTHOR OF "SKETCHES IN THE HUNTING FIELD," ETC., TO WHOM I

OWE MUCH OF MY SUCCESS AS A WRITER, THESE PAGES ARE GRATEFULLY INSCRIBED.

Transcriber's Note: The 15 pages of advertisements preceding the title page have been moved to the end of this book.

INTRODUCTION.

In preparing this work for the press, I may state that it is composed chiefly of a series of papers on horses and their riders, which appeared a short time since in the columns of *The Illustrated Sporting and Dramatic News*. How they originally came to be written and published may not prove uninteresting.

One day, in the middle of February 1880, a goodly company, comprising many thousands of persons, assembled upon the lawn of a nobleman's residence in the vicinity of Dublin; ostensibly for the purpose of hunting, but in reality to gaze at and chronicle the doings of a very distinguished foreign lady, who had lately come to our shores. I was there, of course; and whilst we waited for the Imperial party, I amused myself by watching the moving panorama, and taking notes of costume and effect. Everybody who could procure anything upon which to ride, from a racehorse to a donkey, was there that day, and vehicles of all descriptions blocked up every available inch of the lordly avenues and well-kept carriage-drives.

There is for me so great an attraction in a number of "ladies on horseback" that I looked at them, and at them alone. One sees gentlemen riders every hour in the day, but ladies comparatively seldom; every hunting morning finds about a hundred and fifty mounted males ready for the start, and only on an average about six mounted females, of whom probably not more than the half will ride to hounds. This being the case, I always look most particularly at that which is the greater novelty, nor am I by any means singular in doing so.

On the day of which I write, however, ladies on horseback were by no means uncommon: I should say there were at least two hundred present upon the lawn. Some rode so well, and were so beautifully turned out, that the most hypercritical could find no fault; but of the majority--what can I say? Alas! nothing that would sound at all favourable. Such horses, such saddles, such rusty bridles, such riding-habits, such hats, whips, and gloves; and, above all, such *coiffures*! My very soul was sorry. I could not laugh, as some others were doing. I felt too melancholy for mirth. It seemed to me most grievous that my own sex (many of them so young and beautiful) should be thus held up to ridicule. I asked myself was it thus in other places; and I came to London in the spring, and walked in the Row, and gazed, and took notes, and was not satisfied. Perhaps I was too critical. There was very much to praise, certainly, but there was also much wherewith to find fault. The style of riding was bad; the style of dressing was incomparably worse. The well-got-up only threw into darker shadow the notable defects visible in the forms and trappings of their less fortunate sisterhood. I questioned myself as to how this could be best remedied. Remonstrance was impossible--advice equally so. Why could not somebody write a book for lady equestrians, or a series of papers which might appear in the pages of some fashionable magazine or journal, patronised and read by them? The idea seemed a good one, but I lacked time to carry it out, and so it rested in embryo for many months. Last June, whilst recovering from serious illness, my cherished project returned to my mind. Forbidden to write, and too weak to hold a pen, I strove feebly with a pencil to trace my thoughts upon odd scraps of paper, which I thrust away in my desk without any definite idea as to what should eventually become of them. In July, whilst staying at a country house near Shrewsbury, I one day came upon these shorthand jottings, and, having leisure-time upon my hands, set to work and put them into form. A line to the Editor of *The Illustrated Sporting and Dramatic News*, with whom, I may state, I had had no previous acquaintance, brought an immediate reply, to send my work for consideration. I did so; called upon him by appointment when I came a few days later to London; made all arrangements in a three-minutes interview; and the first of my series of papers appeared shortly after. That they were successful, far beyond their deserts, is to me a proud boast. On their conclusion numerous firms negotiated with me for the copyright: with what result is known; and here to my publishers I tender my best thanks.

In arranging now these writings--put together and brought before the public at a time when I had apparently many years of active life before me--it is to me a melancholy reflection that the things of which they treat are gone from my eyes,--for alas! I can ride no more. Never again may my heart be gladdened with the music of the hounds, or my frame invigorated by the exercise which I so dearly loved. An accident, sudden and unexpected, has deprived me of my strength, and left me to speak in mournful whispers of what was for long my happiest theme. Yet why repine where so much is left? It is but another chapter in our life's history! We love and cling to one pursuit--and it passes from us; then another absorbs our attention,--it, too, vanishes; and so on--perhaps midway to the end--until the "looking back" becomes so filled with saddened memories, that the "looking forward" is alone left. And so we turn our wistful eyes where they might never have been directed, had the prospect behind us been less dark.

A few more words, and I close my preliminary observations and commence my subject. I cannot but be aware, from the nature of the correspondence which has flowed in upon me, that although far the greater number of my readers have agreed with me and entirely coincided in my views, not a few have been found to cavil. Let not such think that I am oblivious of their good intentions because I remain unconvinced by their arguments, and still prefer to maintain my own opinions, which I have not ventured to set forth without mature deliberation, and the most substantial reasons for holding them in fixity of tenure. I have spent some considerable time in turning over in my mind the advisability, or otherwise, of publishing, as a sort of appendix to this volume, a selection from the letters which were printed in *The Illustrated Sporting and Dramatic News* with reference to my writings in that journal. After much deliberation I have decided upon suffering the entire number, with a few trifling exceptions, to appear. They only form a very small proportion of the voluminous correspondence with which the Editor and myself were favoured; but, such as they are, I give them--together with my replies,--not merely because they set forth the views and impressions of various persons upon topics of universal interest, but because I conceive that a large amount of useful information may be gleaned from them, and they may also serve to amuse my lady readers, who will doubtless be interested in the numerous queries which I was called upon to answer. Whether or not I have been able to fight my battles and maintain my cause, must be for others to determine.

I likewise subjoin a little paper on "Hunting in Ireland"--also already published--which brought me many letters: some of them from persons whose word should carry undoubted weight, fully coinciding in and substantiating my views with regard to the cutting up of grass-lands; whilst further on will be found my article entitled "Hunting in America," originally published in *Life*, and copied from that journal into so many papers throughout the kingdom, and abroad, that it is now universally known, and cannot be here presented in the form of a novelty,--but is given for the benefit of those who may not have chanced to meet with it, and for whom the subject of American sports and pastimes may happen to possess interest.

N. P. O'D.

CONTENTS.

PART I.

LEARNING.

CHAPTER I.

CHAPTER II.

CHAPTER III.

PART II.

PARK AND ROAD RIDING.

CHAPTER IV.

CHAPTER V.

PART III.

HUNTING.

CHAPTER VI.

CHAPTER VII.

CHAPTER VIII.

CHAPTER IX.

Selfishness in the Field.--Fording a River.--Shirking a Fence. --Over-riding the Hounds.--Treatment of Tired Hunters.--Bigwig and the Major.--Naughty Bigwig.--Hapless Major 120

CHAPTER X.

CHAPTER XI.

CHAPTER XII.

LADIES ON HORSEBACK.

PART I.

LEARNING.

CHAPTER I.

A POPULAR ERROR.--EXCELLENCE IN RIDING ATTAINABLE WITHOUT ANY YOUTHFUL KNOWLEDGE OF THE ART.--THE EMPRESS OF AUSTRIA.--HER PROFICIENCY.--HER PALACE.--HER OCCUPATIONS.--HER DISPOSITION.--HER THOUGHTS AND OPINIONS. --THE AGE AT WHICH TO LEARN.--COURAGE INDISPENSABLE.--TASTE A NECESSITY.

It is my belief that hints to ladies from a lady, upon a subject which now so universally occupies the female mind--hints, not offered in any cavilling nor carping spirit, but with an affectionate and sisterly regard for the interests of those addressed--cannot fail to be appreciated, and must become popular. Men write very well for men, but in writing for us ladies they cannot, however willing, enter into all the little delicacies and minutiæ of our tastes and feelings, and so half the effect is lost.

I do not purpose entering upon any discussion, nor, indeed, touching more than very lightly upon the treatment and management of the horse. A subject so exhaustive lies totally outside the limits of my pen, and has, moreover, been so ably treated by men of knowledge and experience, as to render one word further respecting the matter almost superfluous. I shall therefore content myself with surmising that the horses with which we may have to do throughout these remarks--be they school-horses, roadsters, or hunters--are at least sound, good-tempered, and properly trained. Their beauty and other attributes we shall take for granted, and not trouble ourselves about.

And now, in addressing my readers, I shall endeavour to do so as though I spoke to each separately, and so shall adopt the term "you," as being at once friendly and concise.

My subject shall be divided into three heads. First the acquirement of the equestrian art; second, road and park riding; third, hunting; with a few hints upon the costume, &c. required for each, and a slight sprinkling of anecdote here and there to enliven the whole.

I shall commence by saying that it is a mistake to imagine that riding, in order to be properly learnt, must be begun in youth: that nobody can excel as a horsewoman who has not accustomed herself to the saddle from a mere child. On the contrary some of the finest *équestriennes* the world has ever produced have known little or nothing of the art until the spring-time of their life was past. Her Imperial Majesty the Empress of Austria, and likewise her sister the ex-Queen of Naples, cared nothing about riding until comparatively late in life. I know little, except through hearsay, of the last-named lady's proficiency in the saddle, but having frequently witnessed that of the former, and having also been favoured with a personal introduction at the gracious request of the Empress, I can unhesitatingly say that anything more superb than her style of riding it would be impossible to conceive. The manner in which she mounts her horse, sits him, manages him, and bears him safely through a difficult run, is something which must be seen to be understood. Her courage is amazing. Indeed, I have been informed that she finds as little difficulty in standing upon a bare-backed steed and driving four others in long reins, as in sitting quietly in one of Kreutzman's saddles. In the circus attached to her palace at Vienna she almost daily performs these feats, and encourages by prizes and evidences of personal favour many of the Viennese ladies who seek to emulate her example. There has been considerable discussion respecting the question of the Empress's womanliness, and the reverse. Ladies have averred--oh, jealous ladies!--that she is *not* womanly; that her style of dressing is objectionable, and that she has "no business to ride without her husband!" These sayings are all open to but one interpretation; ladies are ever envious of each other, more especially of those who excel. The Empress is not only a perfect woman, but an angel of light and goodness. Nor do I say this from any toadyism, nor yet from the gratitude which I must feel for her kindly favour toward myself. I speak as I think and believe. Blessed with a beauty rarely given to mortal, she combines with it a sweetness of character and disposition, a womanly tenderness, and a thoughtful and untiring charity, which deserve to gain for her--as they have gained--the hearts as well as the loving respect and reverence of all with whom she has come in contact.

I was pleased to find, whilst conversing with her, that many of my views about riding were hers also, and that she considered it a pity--as I likewise do--that so many lady riders are utterly spoilt by pernicious and ignorant teaching. I myself am of opinion that childhood is not the best time to acquire the art of riding. The muscles are too young, and the back too weak. The spine is apt to grow crooked, unless a second saddle be adopted, which enables the learner to sit on alternate days upon the off-side of the horse; and to this there are many objections. The best time to learn to ride is about the age of sixteen. All the delicacy to which the female frame is subject during the period from the thirteenth to the fifteenth year has then passed away, and the form is vigorous and strong, and capable of enduring fatigue.

I know it to be a generally accepted idea that riding is like music and literature--the earlier it is learnt the better for the learner, and the more certain the proficiency desired to be attained. This is an entirely erroneous opinion, and one which should be at once discarded. I object, as a rule, to children riding. They cannot do so with any safety, unless put upon horses and ponies which are sheep-like in their demeanour; and from being accustomed to such, and to none other, they are nervous and frightened when mounted upon spirited animals which they feel they have not the strength nor the art to manage, and, being unused to the science of controlling, they suffer themselves to be controlled, and thus extinguish their chance of becoming accomplished horsewomen.

I know ladies, certainly, who ride with a great show of boldness, and tear wildly across country after hounds, averring that they never knew what fear meant: why should they--having ridden from the time they were five years old? Very probably, but the bravery of the few is nothing by which to judge of a system which is, on the whole, pernicious. It is less objectionable for boys, because their shoulders are not apt to grow awry by sitting sideways, as little girls' do; nor are they liable to hang over upon one side; nor have they such delicate frames and weakly fingers to bring to the front. Moreover, if they tumble off, what matter? It does them all the good in the world. A little sticking-plaister and shaking together, and they are all right again. But I confess I *don't like* to see a girl come off. Less than a year ago a sweet little blue-eyed damsel who was prattling by my side as she rode her grey pony along with me, was thrown suddenly and without warning upon the road. The animal stumbled--her tiny hands lacked the strength to pull him together--she was too childish and inexperienced to know the art of retaining her seat. She fell! and the remembrance of uplifting her, and carrying her little hurt form before me upon my saddle to her parents' house, is not amongst the brightest of my memories.

We will assume, then, that you are a young lady in your sixteenth year, possessed of the desire to acquire the art of riding, and the necessary amount of courage to enable you to do so. This latter attribute is an absolute and positive necessity, for a coward will *never* make a horsewoman. If you are a coward, your horse will soon find it out, and will laugh at you; for horses can and do laugh when they what is usually termed "gammon" their riders. Nobody who does not possess unlimited confidence and a determination to know no fear, has any business aspiring to the art. Courage is indispensable, and must be there from the outset. All other difficulties may be got over, but a natural timidity is an insurmountable obstacle.

A cowardly rider labours under a two-fold disadvantage, for she not only suffers from her own cowardice, but actually imparts it to her horse. An animal's keen instinct tells him at once whether his master or his servant is upon his back. The moment your hands touch the reins the horse knows what your courage is, and usually acts accordingly.

No girl should be taught to ride who has not a taste, and a most decided one, for the art. Yet I preach this doctrine in vain; for, all over the world, young persons are forced by injudicious guardians to acquire various accomplishments for which they have no calling, and at which they can never excel. It is just as unwise to compel a girl to mount and manage a horse against her inclination, as it is to force young persons who have no taste for music to sit for hours daily at a piano, or thrust pencils and brushes into hands unwilling to use them. A love for horses, and an earnest desire to acquire the art of riding, are alike necessary to success. An unwilling learner will have a bad seat, a bad method, and clumsy hands upon the reins; whereas an enthusiast will seem to have an innate facility and power to conquer difficulties, and will possess that magic sense of *touch*, and facile delicacy of manipulation, which go so far toward making what are termed "good hands,"--a necessity without which nobody can claim to be a rider.

CHAPTER II.

LEARNER'S COSTUME.--THE BEST TEACHER.--YOUR
BRIDLE.--YOUR SADDLE.-- YOUR STIRRUP.--DANGER
FROM "SAFETY-STIRRUP."--A TERRIBLE SITUATION.
--LEARNING TO RIDE WITHOUT ANY SUPPORT FOR THE
FOOT.

Having now discussed your age, your nerve, and your taste, we
shall say a few words about your costume as a learner. Put on a
pair of strong well-made boots; heels are not objectionable, but
buttons are decidedly so, as they are apt to catch in the stirrup
and cause trouble. Strong chamois riding-trousers, cloth from the
hip down, with straps to fasten under the boots, and soft padding
under the right knee and over the left, to prevent the friction of
the pommels, which, to a beginner, generally causes much pain
and uneasiness. A plain skirt of brown holland, and any sort of
dark jacket, will suit your purpose quite well, for you are only
going to learn; not to show off--yet. Your hat--any kind will
do--must be securely fastened on, and your hair left flowing, for
no matter how well you may fancy you have it fastened, the
motion of the horse will shake it and make it feel unsteady, and
the very first hairpin that drops out, up will go your hand to
replace it, and your reins will be forgotten. As soon as you have
put on a pair of strong loose gloves, and taken a little switch in
your hand, you are ready to mount.

The nicest place in which you can learn is a well-tanned
riding-school or large green paddock, and the nicest person to
teach you is a lady or gentleman friend, who will have the
knowledge and the patience to instruct you. Heaven help the
learner who is handed over to the tender mercies of John, the
coachman, or Jem, the groom! Servants are rarely able to ride a
yard themselves, and their attempt at teaching is proportionately
lame. Your horse having been led out, your attendant looks to
his girthing, &c., as stable servants are not always too particular

respecting these necessary matters.

The pleasantest bridle in which to ride is a plain ring-snaffle. Few horses will go in it; but, remember, I am surmising that yours has been properly trained. By riding in this bridle you have complete control over the movements of your horse--can, in fact, manage him with one hand, and you have the additional advantage of having fewer leathers to encumber and embarrass your fingers. A beginner is frequently puzzled to distinguish between the curb and the snaffle when riding with a double rein, and mistaking one for the other, or pulling equally at both, is apt to cause the horse much unnecessary irritation. It is lamentable to see the manner in which grown men and women, who ought to know so much better, tug and strain at their horses' mouths with an equal pull upon both reins, when riding, as is the custom, in a bit and bridoon. Perhaps of the two they draw the curb the tighter. It is not meant for cruelty--they do not appear to be aware that it *is* cruel: but there is no greater sign of utter ignorance. Horses are not naturally vicious, and very few of them who have had any sort of fair-play in training, really require a curb, or will go as well or pleasantly upon it as if ridden in a snaffle-bridle.

Your saddle is another most important point. Never commence, be your age ever so tender, by riding upon a pad. Accustom yourself from the beginning to the use of a properly constructed saddle, made as straight as a board, seat perfectly level, and scarcely any appearance of a pommel upon the off-side. A leaping-head, or what is commonly termed a third crutch, is, in my opinion, indispensable. To procure a saddle such as I describe you must have it made to order, for those of the present day are all made with something of a dip, which is most objectionable. I do not like the appearance of much stitching about a saddle. It has always appeared to me absurd to see the amount of elaborate embroidery which every old-fashioned saddle carries upon the near flap. Nothing could be more unnecessary than an outlay of labour upon a portion of the article which is always concealed beneath the rider's right leg. There might be some sense, although very little, in decorating the off-side and imparting to it something of an ornamental appearance; but in my opinion there cannot be too much simplicity about everything connected with riding appointments. A plainness, amounting even to severity, is to be preferred before any outward show. Ribbons, and coloured veils, and yellow gloves, and showy flowers are alike objectionable. A gaudy "get up" (to make use of an expressive common-place) is highly to be condemned, and at once stamps the wearer as a person of inferior taste. Therefore avoid it. Let your saddle be, like your personal attire, remarkable only for its perfect freedom from ornament or display. Have it made to suit yourself--neither too weighty, nor yet too small--and if you want to ride with grace and comfort, desire that it be constructed without one particle of the objectionable dip. There is a very old-established and world-noted firm in Piccadilly--Peat & Co.--where you can obtain an article such as I describe, properly made, and of durable materials, at quite a moderate cost. I can say, speaking from experience, that no trouble will be spared to afford you satisfaction, and that the workmanship will be not only lasting, but characterised by that neatness for which I am so strong an advocate. You should ride *on* your saddle, not *in* it, and you must learn to ride from balance or you will never excel, and this you can only do by the use of the level seat. A small pocket on the off-side, and a neat cross strap to support a waterproof, are of course necessary items.

Your stirrup is the next important matter. I strongly disapprove of the old-fashioned slipper, as also of the so-called "safety" stirrup, which is, in my opinion, the fruitful source of many accidents. Half the lamentable mischances with which our ears are from time to time shocked, are due to the pertinacity with which ladies will cling to this murderous safety stirrup. So long as they will persist in doing so, casualties must be looked for and must occur. The padding over the instep causes the foot to become firmly imbedded, and in the event of an accident the consequences are dire, for the mechanism of the stirrup is almost invariably stiff or out of order, or otherwise refuses to act. Mr. Oldacre was, I believe, the inventor of the padded stirrup, and for this we owe him or his memory little thanks, although the gratitude of all lady riders is undoubtedly due to him for his admirable invention and patenting of the third crutch, without which our seat in the saddle would be far less comfortable and less secure.

I dare say that I shall have a large section of aggrieved stirrup-makers coming down upon me with the phials of their wrath for giving publicity to this opinion, but in writing as I have done I merely state my own views, which I deem we are all at liberty to do; and looking upon my readers as friends, I warn them against an article of which I myself have had woful experience. I once purchased a safety stirrup at one of the best houses, and made by one of the best makers. The shopman showed it off to me in gallant style, expatiating upon its many excellencies, and adroitly managing the stiff machinery with his deft fingers, until I was fairly deceived, and gave him a handful of money for what subsequently proved a cause of trouble. I lost more than one good run with hounds through the breaking of this dearly-bought stirrup, having upon one occasion to ride quite a long distance away from the hunt to seek out a forge at which I might undergo repairs. Nor was this the worst, for one day, having incautiously plunged into a bog in my anxiety to be in at the death, my horse got stuck and began to sink, and of course I sought to release myself from him at once; but no, my foot was locked fast in that terrible stirrup, and I could not stir. My position was dreadful, for I had outridden my pilot, my struggling steed was momentarily sinking lower, and the shades of evening were fast closing in. I shudder to think what might have been my fate and that of my gallant horse had not the fox happily turned and led the hunt back along the skirts of the bog, thus enabling my cries for help to be heard by one or two brave spirits who came gallantly to my rescue. I have more than once since then been caught in a treacherous bog when following the chase, but never have I found any difficulty in jumping from my horse's back and helping him to struggle gamely on to the dry land, for I have never since ridden in a safety-stirrup, nor shall I ever be likely to do so again. It may be said, and probably with truth, that my servant had neglected to clean it properly from day to day, and that consequently the spring had got rusted and refused to act. Such may possibly have been the case, but might not the same thing occur to anyone, or at any time? Servants are the same all over the world, and yet you must either trust to them or spend half your time overlooking them in the stable and harness-room, which for a lady is neither agreeable nor correct.

There is nothing so pleasant to ride in as a plain little racing-stirrup, from which the foot is in an instant freed. I have not for a long while back used anything else myself, nor has my foot ever remained caught, even in the most dangerous falls.

I conceive it to be an admirable plan to learn to ride without a stirrup at all. Of course I do not mean by this that a lady should *ever* go out park-riding or hunting *sans* the aid of such an appendage, but she should be taught the necessity of dispensing with it in case of emergency. The benefits arising from such training are manifold. First, it imparts a freedom and independence which cannot otherwise be acquired; secondly, it gives an admirable and sure seat over fences; thirdly, it is an excellent means of learning how to ride from balance; and fourthly, in spite of its apparent difficulties, it is in the end a mighty simplifier, inasmuch as, when the use of the stirrup is again permitted, all seems such marvellously plain sailing, that every obstacle appears to vanish from the learner's path. In short, a lady who can ride fairly well without a support for her foot, must, when such is added, be indeed an accomplished horsewoman. I knew a lady who never made use of a stirrup throughout the whole course of an unusually long life, and who rode most brilliantly to hounds. Few, however, could do this, nor is it by any means advisable, but to be able occasionally to dispense with the support is doubtless of decided benefit.

I have often found my training in this respect stand me in good stead, for it has more than once happened that in jumping a stiff fence, or struggling in a heavy fall, my stirrup-leather has given way, and I have had not alone to finish the run without it, but to ride many miles of a journey homeward.

Nothing could be more wearisome to an untutored horsewoman than a long ride without a stirrup. The weight of her suspended limb becomes after a moment or two most inconvenient and even painful, whilst the trot of the horse occasions her to bump continuously in the saddle,--for the power of rising without artificial aid would appear a sheer impossibility to an ordinary rider whose teaching had been entrusted to an ordinary teacher. I would have you then bear in mind that although I advocate *practising* without the assistance of a stirrup, I am totally against your setting out beyond the limits of your own lawn or paddock without this necessary support.

CHAPTER III.

MOUNTING.--HOLDING THE REINS.--POSITION IN THE
SADDLE.--USE OF THE
WHIP.--TROTTING.--CANTERING.--RIDING FROM
BALANCE.--USE OF THE STIRRUP. --LEAPING.--WHYTE
MELVILLE'S OPINION.

Having now seen that your bridle, saddle, and stirrup are in
proper order, you prepare to mount, and this will probably take
you some time and practice to accomplish gracefully, being quite
an art in itself. Nothing is more atrocious than to see a lady
require a chair to mount her animal, or hang midway against the
side of the saddle when her cavalier gives her the helping hand.
Lay your right hand firmly upon the pommel of your saddle, and
the left upon the shoulder of your attendant, in whose hand you
place your left foot. Have ready some signal sentence, as "Make
ready, go!" or "one, two, three!" Immediately upon pronouncing
the last syllable make your spring, and if your attendant does his
duty properly you will find yourself seated deftly upon your
saddle.

As I have already stated, this requires practice, and you must not
be disappointed if a week or so of failure ensues between trial
and success.

As soon as you are firmly seated, take your rein (which, as I
have said, should be a single one) and adjust it thus. Place the
near side under the little finger of your left hand, and the off one
between your first and second fingers, bringing both in front
toward the right hand, and holding them securely in their place
with the pressure of your thumb. This is merely a hint as to the
simplest method for a beginner to adopt, for there is really no
fixed rule for holding reins, nor must you at all times hold them in
one hand only, but frequently--and always when hunting--put
both hands firmly to your bridle. Anything stiff or stereotyped is to

be avoided. A good rider, such as we hope you will soon become, will change her reins about, and move her position upon the saddle, so as to be able to watch the surrounding scenery--always moving gracefully, and without any abrupt or spasmodic jerkings, which are just as objectionable as the poker-like rigidity which I wish you to avoid. How common it is to see ladies on horseback sitting as though they were afraid to budge a hair, with pinioned elbows and straightly-staring eyes. This is most objectionable; in fact, nothing can be more unsightly. A graceful, easy seat, is a good horsewoman's chief characteristic. She is not afraid of tumbling off, and so she does not look as though she were so; moreover, she has been properly taught in the commencement, and all such defects have been rectified by a careful supervision.

With regard to your whip, it must be held point downwards, and if you have occasion to touch your horse, give it to him down the shoulder, but always with temperance and kindly judgment. I once had a riding-master who desired me to hold my whip balanced in three fingers of my right hand, point upwards, the hand itself being absurdly bowed and the little finger stuck straight out like a wooden projection. My natural good sense induced me to rebel against anything so completely ridiculous, and I quietly asked my teacher why I was to carry my whip in that particular position. His answer was--"Oh, that you may have it ready *to strike your horse on the neck*." Shades of Diana! this is the way our daughters are taught in schools, and we marvel that they show so little for the heaps of money which we hopefully expend upon them.

Being then fairly seated upon your saddle, your skirt drawn down and arranged by your attendant, your reins in your hand and your whip arranged, you must proceed to walk your horse quietly around the enclosure, having first gently drawn your bridle through his mouth. You will feel very strange at first: much as though you were on the back of a dromedary and were completely at his mercy. Sit perfectly straight and erect, but without stiffness. Be careful not to hang over upon either side, and, above all things, avoid the pernicious habit of clutching nervously with the right hand at the off pommel to save yourself from some imaginary danger. So much does this unsightly habit grow upon beginners, that, unless checked, it will follow them through life. I know grown women who ride every day, and the very moment their horse breaks into a canter or a trot they lay a grim grip upon the pommel, and hold firmly on to it until the animal again lapses into a walk. And this they do unconsciously. The habit, given way to in childhood, has grown so much into second nature that to tell them of it would amaze them. I once ventured to offer a gentle remonstrance upon the subject to a lady with whom I was extremely intimate, and she was not only astonished, but so displeased with me for noticing it, that she was never quite the same to me afterwards; and so salutary was the lesson which I then received that I have since gone upon the principle of complete non-interference, and if I saw my fellow *équestriennes* riding gravely upon their horses' heads I would not suggest the rationality of transferring their weight to the saddle. And this theory is a good one, or at least a wise one; for humanity is so inordinately conceited that it will never take a hint kindly, unless asked for; and not always even then.

To sit erect upon your saddle is a point of great importance; if you acquire a habit of stooping it will grow upon you, and it is not only a great disfigurement, but not unfrequently a cause of serious accident, for if your horse suddenly throws up his head, he hits you upon the nose, and deprives you of more blood than you may be able to replace in a good while.

As soon as you can feel yourself quite at home upon your mount, and have become accustomed to its walking motion, your attendant will urge him into a gentle trot. And now prepare yourself for the beginning of sorrows. Your first sensation will be that of being shaken to pieces. You are, of course, yet quite ignorant of the art of rising in your saddle, and the trot of the horse fairly churns you. Your hat shakes, your hair flaps, your elbows bang to your sides, you are altogether miserable. Still, you hold on bravely, though you are ready to cry from the horrors of the situation.

Your attendant, by way of relieving you, changes the trot to a canter, and then you are suddenly transported to Elysium. The motion is heavenly. You have nothing to do but sit close to your saddle, and you are borne delightfully along. It is too ecstatic to last. Alas! it will never teach you to ride, and so you return to the trot and the shaking and the jogging, the horrors of which are worse than anything you have ever previously experienced. You try vainly to give yourself some ease, but fail utterly, and at length dismount--hot, tired, and disheartened.

But against this latter you must resolutely fight. Remember that nothing can be learned without trouble, and by-and-by you will be repaid. It is not everybody who has the gift of perseverance, and it is an invaluable attribute. It is a fact frequently commented upon, not alone by me but by many others also, that if you go for the hiring of a horse to any London livery-stable you will be sent a good-looking beast enough, but he will not be able to trot a yard. Canter, canter, is all that he can do. And why? He is kept for the express purpose of carrying young ladies in the Row, and these young ladies have never learnt to trot. They can dress themselves as vanity suggests in fashionably-cut habits, suffer themselves to be lifted to the saddle, and sit there, looking elegant and pretty, whilst their horse canters gaily down the long ride; but were the animal to break into a trot (which he is far too well tutored to attempt to do), they would soon present the same shaken, dilapidated, dishevelled, and utterly miserable appearance which you yourself do after your first experience of the difficulties which a learner has to encounter.

The art of rising in the saddle is said to have been invented by one Dan Seffert, a very famous steeplechase jockey, who had, I believe, been a riding-master in the days of his youth. If this be true--which there is no reason to doubt--we have certainly to thank him, for it is a vast improvement upon the jog-trot adopted by the cavalry, which, however well it may suit them and impart uniformity of motion to their "line-riding," is not by any means suited to a lady, either for appearances or for purposes of health.

You come up for your next day's lesson in a very solemn mood. You are, in fact, considerably sobered. You had thought it was all plain sailing: it *looked* so easy. You had seen hundreds of persons riding, trotting, and even setting off to hunt, and had never dreamed that there had been any trouble in learning. Now you know the difficulties and what is before you.

You recall your sufferings during your first days upon the ice, or on the rink. How utterly impossible it seemed that you could ever excel; how you tumbled about; how miserably helpless you felt, and how many heavy falls you got! Yet you conquered in the end, and so you will again.

You take courage and mount your steed. First you walk him a little, as yesterday; and then the jolting begins again. How are you ever to get into that rise and fall which you have seen with others, and so much covet? How are you to accomplish it? Only by doing as I tell you, and persevering in it. As your horse throws out his near foreleg press your foot upon your stirrup, in time to lift yourself slightly as his off foreleg is next thrown out. Watch the motion of his legs, press your foot, and at the same time slightly lift yourself from your saddle. For a long while, many days perhaps, it will seem to be all wrong; you have not got into it one bit; you are just as far from it apparently as when you commenced. You are hot and vexed, and you, perhaps, cry with mortification and disappointment, as I have seen many a young beginner do; bitterly worried and disheartened you are, and ready to give up, when, lo! quite suddenly, as though it had come to you by magic and not through your own steady perseverance, you find yourself rising and falling *with* the trot of the horse, and your labours are rewarded.

After this your lessons are a source of delight. You no longer come from them flushed and worried, but joyous and exultant and impatient for the next. You have begun to feel quite brave, and to throw out hints that you are longing for a good ride on the road. You now know how to make your horse trot and canter; the first by a light touch of your whip and a gentle movement of your bridle through his mouth; the second by a slight bearing of the rein upon the near side of his mouth, so as to make him go off upon the right leg, and a little warning touch of your heel. You fancy, in fact, that you are quite a horsewoman, and have already rolled up your hair into a neat knot, and hinted to papa that you should greatly like a habit. But, alas! you have plenty of trouble yet before you, plenty to learn, plenty of falls to get and to bear. At present you can ride fairly well on the straight; but you know nothing of keeping your balance in time of danger. Your horse is very quiet, but if he chanced to put back his ears you would be off.

You are taught to maintain your balance in the following way:--

Your attendant waits until your horse is cantering pretty briskly in a circle from left to right, when he suddenly cracks his whip close to the animal's heels, who immediately swerves and turns the other way. You have had no warning of the movement, and consequently you tumble off, and are put up again, feeling a little shaken and a good deal crestfallen. Most likely you will fall again and again, until you have thoroughly mastered the art of riding from balance.

This is a method I have seen adopted, especially in schools, with considerable success, but it is certainly attended with inconvenience to the learner, and with a goodly portion of the risk from falls which all who ride *must* of necessity run. To ride well from balance is not a thing which can be accomplished in a day, nor a month, nor perhaps a year. Many pass a life-time without practically comprehending the meaning of the term. They ride every day, hold on to the bridle, guide their horses, and trust to chance for the rest; but this is not true horsemanship. It could no more be called *riding* than could a piece of mechanical pianoforte-playing be termed music. When you have, after much difficulty and delay, mastered the obstacles which marred your progress, you will then have the happy consciousness of feeling that however your horse may shy or swerve, or otherwise depart from his good manners, you can sit him with the ease and closeness of a young centaur.

This art of riding from balance is not half sufficiently known. It is one most difficult to acquire, but the study is worth the labour. Nine-tenths of the lady equestrians, and perhaps even a greater number of gentlemen, ride from the horse's head; a detestable practice which cannot be too highly condemned. I must also warn you against placing too much stress upon the stirrup when your horse is trotting. You must bear in mind that the stirrup is intended for a support for the foot--not to be ridden from. By placing your right leg firmly around the up-pommel, and pressing the left knee against the leaping-head, you can accomplish the rise in your saddle with slight assistance from the stirrup; and this is the proper way to ride. The lazy, careless habit into which many women fall, of resting the entire weight of the body upon the stirrup, not only frequently causes the leathers to snap at most inconvenient times, but is the lamentable cause of half the sore backs and ugly galls from which poor horses suffer so severely.

Having at length perfected yourself in walking, trotting, cantering, and riding from balance, you have only to acquire the art of leaping--and then you will be finished, so far as teaching can make you so. Experience must do the rest.

It is a good thing, when learning, to mount as many different horses as you possibly can; always, of course, taking care that they are sufficiently trained not to endeavour to master you. Horses vary immensely in their action and gait of going: so much so, that if you do not accustom yourself to a variety you will take your ideas from one alone, and will, when put upon a strange animal, find yourself completely at sea.

Do not suffer anything to induce you to take your first leap over a bar or pole similar to those used in schools. The horse sees the daylight under it, knows well that it is a sham, goes at it unwillingly, does not half rise to it, drops his heels when in the air, and knocks it down with a crash,--only to do the same thing a second time, and a third, and a fourth also, if urged to do that which he despises.

Choose a nice little hurdle about two feet high, well interwoven with gorse; trot your horse gently up to it, and let him see what it is; then, turn him back and send him at it, sitting close glued to your saddle, with a firm but gentle grip of your reins, and your hands held low. To throw up the hands is a habit with all beginners, and should at once be checked. Fifty to one you will stick on all right, and, if you come off, why it's many a good man's case, and you must regard it as one of the chances of war.

The next day you may have the gorse raised another half-foot above the hurdle, and so on by degrees, until you can sit with ease over a jump of five feet. Always bear in mind to keep your hands quite down upon your horse's withers, and never interfere with his mouth. Sit well back, leave him his head, and he will not make a mistake. Of course, I am again surmising that he has been properly trained, and that you alone are the novice. To put a learner upon an untrained animal would be a piece of folly, not to say of wickedness, of which we hope nobody in this age of enlightenment would dream of being guilty. In jumping a fence or hurdle do not leave your reins quite slack; hold them lightly but firmly, as your horse should jump against his bridle, but do not pull him. A gentle support is alone necessary.

That absurd and vulgar theory about "lifting a horse at his fences," so freely affected by the ignorant youth of the present day, cannot be too strongly deprecated. That same "lifting" has broken more horses' shoulders and more *asses'* necks than anything else on record. A good hunter with a bad rider upon his back will actually shake his head free on coming up to a fence. He knows that he cannot do what is expected of him if his mouth is to be chucked and worried, any more than you or I could under similar circumstances, and so he asserts his liberty. How often, in a steeplechase, one horse early deprived of his rider will voluntarily go the whole course and jump every obstacle in perfect safety, even with the reins dangling about his legs, yet never make a mistake; whilst a score or so of compeers will be tumbling at every fence. And why? The answer is plain and simple. The free horse has his head, and his instinct tells him where to put his feet; whereas the animals with riders upon their backs are dragged and pulled and sawn at, until irritation deprives them of sense and sight, and, rushing wildly at their fences (probably getting another tug at the moment of rising), they fall, and so extinguish their chance of a win.

I do not, of course, in saying this, mean for a moment to question the judgment and horsemanship of very many excellent jockeys, whose ability is beyond comment and their riding without reproach. I speak of the rule, not of the few exceptions.

Half the horses who fall in the hunting-field are thrown down by their riders; this is a fact too obvious to be contradicted. Men over-riding their horses, treating them with needless cruelty, riding them when already beaten: these are the fruitful causes of falls in the field, together with that most objectionable practice of striving to "lift" an animal who knows his duties far better than the man upon his back. It is a pity, and my heart has often bled to see how the noblest of God's created things is ill-treated and abused by the human brute who styles himself the master. It is, indeed, a disgrace to our humanity that this priceless creature, given to a man with a mind highly wrought, sensitive, yearning for kindness, and capable of appreciating each word and look of the being whose willing slave it is, should be treated with cruelty, and in too many cases regarded but as a sort of machine to do the master's bidding. Who has not seen, and mourned to see, the tired, patient horse, spurred and dragged at by a remorseless rider, struggling gamely forward in the hunting-field, with bleeding mouth and heaving, bloody flanks, to enable a cruel task-master to see the end of a second run, and even of a third, after having carried him gallantly through a long and intricate first? It is a piece of inhumanity which all humane riders see and deplore every day throughout the hunting season. We cannot stop it, but we can speak against it and write it down, and discountenance it in every possible way, as we are all bound to do. Why will not men be brought to see that in abusing their horses they are compassing their own loss? that in taxing the powers of a beaten animal they are riding for a fall, and are consequently endangering the life which God has given them?

There is much to be learnt in the art of fencing besides hurdle-leaping. A good timber-jumper will often take a ditch or drain in a very indifferent manner. I have seen a horse jump a five-barred gate in magnificent style, yet fall short into a comparatively narrow ditch; and *vice versâ*; therefore, various kinds of jumps must be kept up, persevered in, and kept constantly in practice. Two things must always be preserved in view; never sit loosely in your saddle, and always ride well from balance, never from your horse's head. In taking an up jump leave him abundance of head-room, and sit *well* back, lest in his effort he knock you in the face. If the jump is a down one--what is known as an "ugly drop"--follow the same rules; but, when your horse is landing, give him good support from the bridle, as, should the ground be at all soft or marshy, he might be apt to peck, and so give you an ugly fall.

It is a disputed point whether or not horses like jumping. I am inclined to coincide in poor Whyte-Melville's opinion that they do not. He was a good authority upon most subjects connected with equine matters, and so he ought to know; but of one thing I am positively certain: they abhor schooling. However a horse may tolerate or even enjoy a good fast scurry with hounds, there can be no doubt that he greatly dislikes being brought to his fences in cold blood. He has not, when schooling, the impetus which sends him along, nor the example or excitement to be met with in the hunting-field. The horse is naturally a timid animal, and this is why he so frequently stops short at his fences when schooling. He mistrusts his own powers. When running with hounds he is borne along by speed and by excitement, and so goes skying over obstacles which appal him when trotted quietly to them on a schooling day. It is just the difference which an actor feels between a chilling rehearsal and the night performance, when the theatre is crowded and the clapping of hands and the shouting of approving voices lend life and spirit to the part he plays.

You will probably get more falls whilst schooling than ever you will get in the hunting-field, but a few weeks' steady practice over good artificial fences or a nice natural country, will give you a firm seat and an amount of confidence which will stand to you as friends.

PART II.

PARK AND ROAD RIDING.

CHAPTER IV.

HOW TO DRESS.--A COUNTRY-GIRL'S IDEAS UPON THE SUBJECT.--HOW TO PUT ON YOUR RIDING-GEAR.--HOW TO PRESERVE IT.--FIRST ROAD-RIDE.--BACKING. --REARING, AND HOW TO PREVENT IT.

Having now mastered the art of riding, you will of course be desirous of appearing in the parks and on the public roadways, and exhibiting the prowess which it has cost you so much to gain.

For your outfit you will require, in addition to the articles already in your possession, a nice well-made habit of dark cloth. If you are a very young girl, grey will be the most suitable; if not, dark blue. If you live in London, pay a visit to Mayfair, and get Mr. Wolmershausen to make it for you; if in Dublin, Mr. Scott, of Sackville Street, will do equally well; indeed, for any sort of riding-gear, ladies' or gentlemen's, he is not to be excelled. If you are not within easy distance of a city, go to the best tailor you can, and give him directions, which he must not be above taking. Skirt to reach six inches below the foot, well shaped for the knee, and neatly shotted at end of hem just below the right foot; elastic band upon inner side, to catch the left toe, and to retain the skirt in its place. It should be made tight and spare, without *one inch* of superfluous cloth; jacket close-fitting, but sufficiently easy to avoid even the suspicion of being squeezed; sleeves perfectly tight, except at the setting on, where a slight puffiness over the shoulder should give the appearance of increased width of chest. No braiding nor ornamentation of any sort to appear. A small neat linen collar, upright shape, with cuffs to correspond, should be worn with the habit, no frilling nor fancy work being admissible--the collar to be fastened with a plain gold or silver stud.

The nicest hat to ride in is an ordinary silk one, much lower than they are usually made, and generally requiring to be manufactured purposely to fit and suit the head. Of course, if you are a young girl, the melon shape will not be unsuitable, but the other is more in keeping, more becoming, and vastly more economical in the end, although few can be induced to believe this. It is the custom in many households to purchase articles for their cheapness, without any regard to quality or durability, and this you should endeavour to avoid. Speaking from experience, the best things are always the cheapest. I pay from a guinea to a guinea and a half for a good silk hat, and find that it wears out four felt ones of the quality usually sold at ten and sixpence. There is no London house at which you can procure better articles or better value than at Lincoln, Bennett, & Co., Sackville Street, Piccadilly. For nearly half a century they have been the possessors of an admirable contrivance, which should be seen to be appreciated, by which not alone is the size of the head ascertained, but its precise shape is definitely marked and suited, thus avoiding all possibility of that distressing pressure upon the temples, which is a fruitful source of headache and discomfort to so many riders. Hats made at this firm require no elastics--if it be considered desirable to dispense with such--as the fit is guaranteed. Never wear a veil on horseback, except it be a black one, and nothing with a border looks well. A plain band of spotted net, just reaching below the nostrils, and gathered away into a neat knot behind, is the most *distingué*. Do not wear anything sufficiently long to cover the mouth, or it will cause you inconvenience on wet and frosty days. For dusty roads a black gauze veil will be found useful, but avoid, as you would poison, every temptation to wear even the faintest scrap of colour on horseback. All such atrocities as blue and green veils have happily long since vanished, but, even still, a red bow, a gaudy flower stuck in the button-hole, and, oh, horror of horrors! a pocket handkerchief appearing at an opening in the bosom, looking like a miniature fomentation--these still occasionally shock the eyes of sensitive persons, and cause us to marvel at the wearer's bad taste.

I was once asked to take a young lady with me for a ride in the park, to witness a field-day, or polo match, or something or another of especial interest which happened to be going forward. I would generally prefer being asked to face a battery of Zulus rather than act as *chaperone* to young lady *équestriennes*, who are usually ignorant of riding, and insufferably badly turned out. However, upon this occasion I could not refuse. The lady's parents were kind, amiable country folks, who had invested a portion of their wealth in sending their daughter up to town to get lessons from a fashionable riding-master, and to ride out with whomsoever might be induced to take her.

Well, the young lady's horse was the first arrival: a hired hack--usual style; bones protruding--knees well over--rusty bridle--greasy reins--dirty girths--and dilapidated saddle, indifferently polished up for the occasion.

The young lady herself came next, stepping daintily out of a cab, as though she were quite mistress of the situation. Ye gods! What a get up! I was positively electrified. Her habit--certainly well made--was of bright blue cloth, with worked frills at the throat and wrists. She wore a brilliant knot of scarlet ribbon at her neck, and a huge bouquet in her button-hole. Her hat was a silk one, set right on the back of her head, with a velvet rosettte and steel buckle in front, and a long veil of grey gauze streaming out behind. When we add orange gloves, and a riding-whip with a gaudy tassel appended to it, you have the details of a costume at once singular and unique.

I did not at first know whether to get a sudden attack of the measles or the toothache, and send her out with my groom to escort her, but discarding the thought as ill-natured, I compromised matters by bringing her to my own room, and effecting alterations in her toilet which soon gave her a more civilised appearance. I set the hat straight upon her head, and bound it securely in its place, removed from it the gauze and buckle, and tied on one of my own plain black veils of simple spotted net. I could not do away with the frillings, for they were stitched on as though they were never meant to come off; but the red bow I replaced with a silver arrow, threw away the flowers, removed the whip-tassel, and substituted a pair of my own gloves for the cherished orange kid. Then we set out.

I wanted to go a quiet way to the park, so as to avoid the streets of the town, but she would not have it. Nothing would do that girl but to go bang through the most crowded parts of the city, the hired hack sliding over the asphalte, and the rider (all unconscious of her danger) bowing delightedly to her acquaintances as she passed along. Poor girl! that first day out of the riding-school was a gala day for her.

The nicest gloves for riding are pale cream leather, worked thickly on the backs with black. A few pairs of these will keep you going, for they clean beautifully. A plain riding-whip *without* a tassel, and a second habit of dark holland if you live in the country, will complete your necessary outfit.

I shall now give you a few hints as to the best method of putting on your riding gear, and of preserving the same after rain or hard weather. Your habit-maker will, of course, put large hooks around the waist of your bodice, and eyes of corresponding size attached to the skirt, so that both may be kept in their place, but if you have been obliged to entrust your cloth to a country practitioner, who has neglected these minor necessaries, be sure you look to them yourself, or you will some day find that the opening of your skirt is right at your back, and that the place shaped out for your knee has twisted round until it hangs in unsightly crookedness in front of the buttons of your bodice.

Let it be a rule with you to avoid using any pins. Put two or three neat stitches in the back of your collar, so as to affix it to your jacket, having first measured to see that the ends shall meet exactly evenly in front, where you will fasten them neatly with a stud. The ordinary system of placing one pin at the back of the collar and one at either end is much to be deprecated. Frequently one of these pins becomes undone, and then the discomfort is incalculable, especially if, as often occurs, you are out for a long day, and nobody happens to be able to accommodate you with another.

Pinning cuffs is also a reprehensible habit, for the reason just stated. Two or three little stitches where they will not show, upon the inner side of the sleeve, will hold the cuff securely in its place and prevent it turning round or slipping up or down, any of which will be calculated to cause discomfort to the rider.

It is not a bad method, either, to stitch a small button at the back of the neck of the jacket, upon the inner side, upon which the collar can be secured, fastening the cuffs in the same manner to buttons attached to the inner portion of each sleeve. In short, anything in the shape of a device which will check the unseemly habit of using a multiplicity of pins, may be regarded as a welcome innovation, and at once adopted.

It is a good plan, when you undress from your ride, to ascertain whether your collar and cuffs are sufficiently clean to serve you another day, and if they are not, replace them at once by fresh ones; for it may happen that when you go to attire yourself for your next ride, you may he too hurried to look after what should always be a positive necessity, namely, perfectly spotless linen.

There is a material, invented in America and as yet but little known amongst us here, which is invaluable to all who ride. It is called Celluloid, and from it collars, cuffs, and shirt-fronts are manufactured which resemble the finest and whitest linen, yet which never spot, never crush, never become limp, and never require washing, save as one would wash a china saucer, in a basin of clear water, using a fine soft towel for the drying process. I do not know the nature of the composition, but I can certainly bear testimony to its worth, and being inexpensive as well as convenient, it cannot fail, when known, to become highly popular.

The adjusting of your hat is another important item. Stitch a piece of black elastic (the single-cord round kind is the best) from one side--the inner one of course--to the other, of just sufficient length to catch well beneath your hair. This elastic you can stretch over the leaf of your hat at the back, and then, when the hat is on and nicely adjusted to your taste in front, you have only to put back your hand and bring the band of elastic deftly under your hair. The hat will then be immovable, and the elastic will not show. In fastening your veil, a short steel pin with a round black head is the best. The steel slips easily through the leaf of the hat, and the head, being glossy and large, is easily found without groping or delay, whenever you may desire to divest yourself of it.

I shall now tell you how to proceed with the various items of your toilet on coming home, after being overtaken by stress of weather. No matter how wealthy you may be, or how many servants you may be entitled to keep, always look after these things yourself.

Hang the skirt of your habit upon a clothes-horse, with a stick placed across inside to extend it fully. Leave it until thoroughly dry, and then brush carefully. The bodice must be hung in a cool dry place, but never placed near the fire, or the cloth will shrink, and probably discolour.

Dip your veil into clear cold water, give it one or two gentle squeezes, shake it out, and hang it on a line, spreading it neatly with your fingers, so that it may take no fold in the drying.

Your hat comes next. Dip a fine small Turkey sponge, kept for the purpose and freed from sand, into a basin of lukewarm water, and draw it carefully around the hat. Repeat the process, going over every portion of it, until crown, leaf, and all are thoroughly cleansed; then hang in a cool, airy place to dry. In the morning take a soft brush, which use gently over the entire surface, and you will have a perfectly new hat. No matter how shabby may have been your headpiece, it will be quite restored, and will look all the better for its washing. This is one of the chief advantages of silk hats. Do not omit to brush after the washing and drying process, or your hat will have that unsightly appearance of having been ironed, which is so frequently seen in the hunting-field, because gentlemen who are valeted on returning from their sport care nothing about the management of their gear, but leave it all to the valet, who gives the hat the necessary washing, but is too lazy or too careless to brush it next day, and his master takes it from his hand and puts it on without ever noticing its unsightliness. Sometimes it is the master himself whose clumsy handiwork is to blame; but be it master or servant, the result is too often the same.

Should your gloves be thoroughly, or even slightly wetted, stretch them upon a pair of wooden hands kept for the purpose, and if they are the kind which I have recommended to you--I mean the best quality of double-stitched cream leather--they will be little the worse.

Having now, I think, exhausted the subject of your clothing, and given you all the friendly hints in my power, I am ready to accompany you upon your first road ride.

Go out with every confidence, accompanied of course by a companion or attendant, and make up your mind never to be caught napping, but to be ever on the alert. You must not lose sight of the fact that a bird flitting suddenly across, a donkey's head laid without warning against a gate, a goat's horns appearing over a wall, or even a piece of paper blown along upon the ground, may cause your horse to shy, and if you are not sitting close at the time, woe betide you! Always remember the rule of the road, keep to your left-hand side, and if you have to pass a vehicle going your way, do so on the right of it. Never neglect this axiom, no matter how lonely and deserted the highway may appear, for recollect that if you fail to comply with it, and that any accident chances to occur, you will get all the blame, and receive no compensation.

Never trot your horse upon a hard road when you have a bit of grass at the side on which you can canter him. Even if there are only a few blades it will be sufficient to take the jar off his feet.

If you meet with a hill or high bridge, trot him up and walk him quietly down the other side. If going down a steep decline, sit well back and leave him his head, at the same time keeping a watchful hand upon the rein for fear he should chance to make a false step, that you may be able to pull him up; but do not hold him tightly in, as many timid riders are apt to do, thus hobbling his movements and preventing him seeing where he is to put his feet. If he has to clamber a steep hill with you, leave him unlimited head-room, for it is a great ease to a horse to be able to stretch his neck, instead of being held tightly in by nervous hands, which is frequently the occasion of his stumbling.

Should your horse show temper and attempt to back with you, leave him the rein, touch him lightly with your heel, and speak encouragingly to him; should he persist, your attendant must look to the matter; but a horse who possesses this dangerous vice should never be ridden by a lady. I have surmised that yours has been properly trained, and doubtless you might ride for the greater portion of a lifetime without having to encounter a decided jibber, but it is as well to be prepared for all emergencies. Should a horse at any time rear with you, throw the rein loose, sit close, and bring your whip sharply across his flank. If this is not effectual, you may give him the butt-end of it between the ears, which will be pretty sure to bring him down. This is a point, however, upon which I write with considerable reserve, for many really excellent riders find fault with the theory set forth and adopted by me. One old sportsman in particular shows practically how seriously he objects to it by suffering himself to be tumbled back upon almost daily by a vicious animal, in preference to adopting coercive measures for his own safety.

My reasons for striking a rearing horse are set forth with tolerable clearness in one of the letters which form an appendix to this volume; but, although I do it myself, I do not undertake the responsibility of advising others to do likewise, especially if a nervous timidity form a portion of their nature. I am strongly of opinion, however, that decisive measures are at times an absolute necessity, and that the most effectual remedy for an evil is invariably the best to adopt. I have heard it said by two very eminent horsemen that to break a bottle of water between the ears of a rearing animal is an excellent and effectual cure. Perhaps it may be--and, on such authority, we must suppose that it is--but I should not care to be the one to try it, although I consider no preventive measure too strong to adopt when dealing with so dangerous a vice. A horse may be guilty of jibbing, bolting, kicking, or almost any other fault, through nervousness or timidity, but rearing is a vicious trick, and must be treated with prompt determination. It would be useless to speak encouragingly to a rearer; he is vexing you from vice, not from nervousness, and so he needs no reassurance--do not waste words upon him, but bring him to his senses with promptitude, or whilst you are dallying he may tumble back upon you, and put remonstrance out of your power for some time to come, if not for ever. In striking him, if you do so, do not indulge in the belief that you are safe because he drops quickly upon his fore-legs, but on the contrary, be fully prepared for the kick or buck which will be pretty sure to follow, and which (unless watched for) will be likely to unseat even a most skilful rider. Both rearing and plunging may, however, be effectually prevented by using the circular bit and martingale, procurable at Messrs. Davis, saddlers, 14, Strand, London. This admirable contrivance should be fitted above the mouthpiece of an ordinary snaffle or Pelham bridle. It is infinitely before any other which I have seen used for the same purpose, has quite a separate headstall, and should be put on and arranged before the addition of the customary bridle. Being secured to the breastplate by a standing martingale, it requires no reins.

CHAPTER V.

RUNNING AWAY.--THREE DANGEROUS ADVENTURES.--HOW TO ACT WHEN PLACED IN CIRCUMSTANCES OF PERIL.--HOW TO RIDE A PULLER.--THROUGH THE CITY.--TO A MEET OF HOUNDS.--BOASTFUL LADIES.--A BRAGGART'S RESOURCE.

In the event of a horse running away, you must of course be guided by circumstances and surroundings, but my advice always is, if you have a fair road before you, let him go. Do not attempt to hold him in, for the support which you afford him with the bridle only helps the mischief. Leave his head quite loose, and when you feel him beginning to tire--which he will soon do without the support of the rein--flog him until he is ready to stand still. I warrant that a horse treated thus, especially if you can breast him up hill, will rarely run away a second time. He never forgets his punishment, nor seeks to put himself in for a repetition of it.

I have been run away with three times in my life, but never a second time by the same horse. It may amuse you to hear how I escaped upon each occasion.

The first time, I was riding a beautiful little thoroughbred mare, which a dear lady friend--now, alas! dead--had asked me to try for her. The mare had been a flat-racer, and, having broken down in one of her trials, had been purchased at a cheap rate, being still possessed of beauty and a considerable turn of speed.

Well, we got on splendidly together for an hour or so on the fifteen acres, Phoenix Park, but, when returning homewards, some boys who were playing close by struck her with a ball on the leg. In a second she was off like the wind, tearing down the long road which leads from the Phoenix to the gates. She had the bit between her teeth, and held it like a vice. My only fear was lest she should lose her footing and fall, for the roadway was covered from edge to edge with new shingle. On she went in her mad career, amidst the shrieks of thousands, for the day was Easter Monday, and the park was crowded. Soldiers, civilians, lines of policemen strove to form a barrier for her arrest. In vain! She knocked down some, fled past others, and continued her headlong course.

All this time I was sitting as if glued to my saddle. At the mare's first starting I had endeavoured to pull her up, but finding that this was hopeless, I left the rein loose upon her neck. Having then no support for her head, she soon tired, and the instant I felt her speed relaxing I took up my whip and punished her within an inch of her life. I *made* her go when she wanted to stop, and only suffered her to pull up just within the gates, where she stood covered with foam and trembling in every limb.

Her owner subsequently told me that during the three years which she afterwards kept her she never rode so biddable a mare.

I must not forget to mention the comic side of the adventure as well as the more serious. It struck me as being particularly ludicrous upon that memorable occasion that an old gentleman, crimson with wrath, actually attacked my servant in the most irate manner because he had not clattered after me during the progress of the mare's wild career. "How dare you, sir," cried this irascible old gentleman, "how dare you attempt to neglect your young lady in this cowardly manner?" Nor was his anger at all appeased when informed that I as a matron was my own care-taker, and that my attendant had strict injunctions *not* to follow me in the event of my horse being startled or running away.

My next adventure was much more serious, and occurred also within the gates of the Phoenix Park.

Some troops were going through a variety of manoeuvres preparing for a field-day, and a knot of them had been posted behind and around a large tree with fixed bayonets in their hands. Suddenly they got the order to move, and at the same instant the sun shone out and glinted brilliantly upon the glittering steel. I was riding a horse which had lately been given me; a fine, raking chestnut, with a temper of his own to manage. He turned like a shot, and sped away at untold speed. I had no open space before me; therefore I durst not let him go. It was an enclosed portion of the park, thickly studded with knots of trees, and I knew that if he bore me through one of these my earthly career would most probably be ended. I strove with all the strength and all the art which I possessed to pull him up. It was of no use. I might as well have been pulling at an oak-tree; it only made him go the faster.

Happily my presence of mind remained. I saw at once that my only chance was to breast him against the rails of the cricket-ground, and for these I made straight, prepared for the shock and for the turn over which I knew must inevitably follow. He dashed up to the rails, and when within a couple of inches of them he swerved with an awful suddenness, which, only that I was accustomed to ride from balance, must have at once unseated me, and darted away at greater speed than ever. Right before me was a tree, one heavy bough of which hung very low--and straight for this he made, nor could I turn his course. I knew my fate, and bent on a level with my saddle, but not low enough, for the branch caught me in the forehead and sent me reeling senseless to the ground.

I soon got over the shock, although my arm (which was badly torn by a projecting branch) gave me some trouble after; but the bough was cut down the next day by order of the Lord

Lieutenant, and the park-rangers still point out the spot as the place where "the lady was nearly killed."

My third runaway was a hunting adventure, and occurred only a few months since.

I had a letter one morning from an old friend, informing me that a drag-hunt was to take place about thirty miles from Dublin to finish the season with the county harriers, and that he, my friend, wished very much that I would come down in my habit by the mid-day train and ride a big bay horse of his, respecting which he was desirous of obtaining my opinion. I never take long to make up my mind, so, after a glance at my tablets, which showed me that I was free for the day, I donned my habit, and caught the specified train.

At the station at the end of my journey I found the big bay saddled and awaiting me, and having mounted him I set off for the kennels, from a field near which the drag was to be run. I took the huntsman for a pilot, knowing that the servant, who was my attendant, was rather a duffer at the chase.

The instant that the hounds were laid on and the hunt started, my big mount commenced to pull hard, and by the time the first fence was reached his superior strength had completely mastered mine. He was pulling like a steam-engine, head down, ears laid backward, neck set like iron. My blistered hands were powerless to hold him. He rushed wildly at the fence, and striking the horse of a lady who was just landing over it, turned him and his rider a complete somersault! I subsequently learned that the lady escaped unhurt, but I could not at the moment pause to inquire, for my huge mount, clearing the jump and ten feet beyond it, completely took head, and bore me away from the field

Over park, over pale, Through bush, through briar,

until my head fairly reeled, and I felt that some terrible calamity must ensue.

Happily he was a glorious fencer, or I must have perished, for he jumped every obstacle with a rush; staked fences, wide ditches--so wide that he landed over them on his belly--tangled gorse, and branches of rivers swollen by recent rains; he flew them all. At length, when my strength was quite exhausted and my dizzy brain utterly powerless and confused, I beheld before me a stone wall, a high one, with heavy coping-stones upon the top. At this I resolved to breast him, and run my chance for life or death in the turn over, which, from the pace at which we were approaching it, I knew must be a mighty one. In a moment we were up to it and, with a cry to heaven for mercy, I dug him with my spur and sent him at it. To my utter astonishment, for the wall was six and a half feet high, he put down his head, rushed at it, cleared it without ever laying a shoe upon the topmost stones, and landed with a frightful slip and clatter, but still safely on his feet--where? in the midst of a farm-yard.

Were it not that this adventure actually occurred to myself, I should be strongly tempted to question its authenticity. That there are horses--especially Irish ones--quite capable of compassing such a jump, there cannot be the slightest doubt; but I have never before or since seen one who could do it without being steadied as he approached the obstacle. In the ordinary course of events a runaway steed would strike it with his head and turn over,--which was what I expected and desired--but no such thing occurred, and to the latest hour of my life it must remain a mystery to me that upon the momentous occasion in question neither horse nor rider was injured, nor did any accident ensue. Nothing more disastrous than a considerable disturbance in the farm-yard actually occurred; but it was indeed a mighty one.

Such a commotion amongst fowls was surely never witnessed; the ducks quacked, the turkeys screeched, the hens ran hither and thither; two pigs, eating from a trough close by, set up a most terrific squalling, dogs barked, and two or three women, who were spreading clothes upon a line, added to the general confusion by flinging down the garments with which they had been busy and taking to their heels, shrieking vociferously. In the meantime the big bay, perceiving that he had run to the end of his tether, stood snorting and foaming, looking hither and thither in helpless amazement and dismay; whilst I, relieved at length of my anxiety, burst first into tears, and then into shouts of hearty laughter, as I fully took in the absurdity of the situation.

After a considerable delay one of the women was induced to come forward and listen to a recital of my adventure; and the others, being assured that "the baste" would not actually devour them, came near me also, and we held an amicable council as to the possibility of my ever getting out, for the gates were locked, and the owner of the property was away at a fair in the neighbouring town and had the key stowed away in his pocket. To jump the wall again was impracticable. No horse that ever was foaled could do it in cool blood; nor was I willing to risk the experiment, even if my steed made no objection.

At length we decided upon the only plan. I dismounted, and, taking the rein over my arm, led my mighty hunter across the yard, induced him to stoop his head to enter by a back door through a passage in the farmhouse, and from thence through the kitchen and front door, out on to the road. I have a cheerful recollection of an old woman, who was knitting in the chimney-corner, going off into screams and hysterics as I and my big steed walked in upon her solitude, a loose shoe and a very audible blowing making the entrance of my equine companion even more *prononcé* than it would otherwise have been. The poor old creature flung down her needles, together with the cat which had been quietly reposing in her lap, and kicking up her feet yelled and bellowed at the top of a very discordant voice. It took the combined efforts of all four women to pacify her, and she was still shrieking long after I had mounted the big bay and ridden him back to inform his owner of how charmingly he had behaved.

I have now told you three anecdotes, partly for your amusement and partly for your instruction; but I would not have you think that it would be at all times and under all circumstances a wise thing to ride a runaway horse against so formidable an obstacle as a stone wall. Mine was, I hope, an exceptional case. When the animal was led down to meet me at the station, I saw, not without misgiving, that I was destined to ride in a so-called "safety-stirrup," and at the time when he took head with me my foot was fixed as in a vice in this dangerous and horrible trap, from which I could not succeed in releasing it. Feeling that my brain was whirling, and that I could not longer maintain my seat in the saddle, I rode for an overthrow, which I deemed infinitely better than being dragged by the foot over an intricate country, and most probably having my brains scattered by a pair of crashing heels. If a horse should at any time run away with you, keep your seat whilst you *can* do so, and whilst you have anything of a fair road before you; but if there is any danger of your being thrown or losing your seat whilst your foot is caught, then by all means ride for a fall; put your horse at something that will bring him down, and when he *is* down struggle on to his head, that he may not rise until somebody has come to your assistance. Of course the experiment is fraught with excessive danger, but it is not *certain* death, as the other alternative must undoubtedly be. I cannot, however, wish you better than to hope most fervently that you may never be placed in a position which would necessitate your making a choice between two such mighty evils. Avoid riding strange horses. No matter how accomplished a horsewoman you may become, do not be too ready to comply with the request to try this or that unknown mount. I have done it myself, often, and probably shall again;[1]

but my experience prompts me to warn others against a practice which is frequently fraught with danger to a lady. A horse knows quite well when a strange or timid rider gets upon his back, and if he does not kill you outright, he will probably make such a "hare" of you as will not be at all agreeable, either for yourself or for the lookers-on.

[1] This was written previous to the accident which has disabled me.

Whenever you take a young horse upon grass, whether he be a stranger to you or otherwise, be prepared for a certain show of friskiness which he does not usually exhibit upon the road. The soft springy turf beneath his feet imbues him with feelings of hilarity which he finds himself powerless to resist, and so you, his rider, must prepare for his little vagaries. He will, most probably, in the first place try a succession of bucks, and for these you must prepare by sitting very close to your saddle, your knee well pressed against the leaping-head, and your figure erect, but not thrown back, as the shock, or shocks to your spine would in such a case be not only painful but positively dangerous, and should therefore be carefully avoided. He will next be likely to romp away, pulling you much harder than is at all agreeable, and seemingly inclined to take head with you altogether. As a remedy against this you must neither yield to him nor pull against him. I have heard fairly good riders advocate by turns both systems of management, especially the former; indeed, the expression, "Drop your hands to him," has become so general amongst teachers of the equestrian art, that it has almost passed into a proverb. I do not advocate it, nor do I deem it advisable ever to pull against a pulling horse. When an animal tries to forereach you, you should neither give up to him nor yet pull one ounce against him. Close your fingers firmly upon the reins and keep your arms perfectly motionless, your hands well down, without giving or taking one quarter of an inch. In a stride or two he will be sure to yield to your hand, at which moment you should immediately yield to him, and his wondrous powers of intelligence will soon enable him to discern that you are not to be trifled with. Were you to give up to him when he rushes away or romps with his head he would very soon be going all abroad, and would give you a vast amount of trouble to pull him into proper form. Above all things, keep clear of trees, of which I myself have an unbounded dread. Should you have occasion to ride through a city, give your eyes and attention to your horse, and not to passing acquaintances, for in the present dangerous tangle of tramlines, slippery pavements, and ill-driven vehicles, it will require all your energies to bring you safely through. Never trot your horse through a town or city: walk him quietly through such portion of it as you have to pass, and leave him abundant head-room, that his intelligence may pick out a way for his own steps.

A very nice ride for a lady is to a meet of the hounds, if such should occur within reasonable distance, say from four to eight miles. The sight is a very pretty one, and there is not any reason why you should not thoroughly enjoy it; but having only ridden to see the meet, you must be careful not to interfere with, nor get in the way of those about to ride the run. Nothing is more charming than to see three or four ladies, nicely turned out, arrive to grace the meet with their presence, but nothing is more abominable than the same number of amazons coming galloping up in full hunting toggery, although without the least idea of hunting, and rushing hither and thither, frightening the hounds and getting in everybody's way, as though they were personages of the vastest possible importance, and meant to ride with a skill not second to that of the Nazares. Such women are the horror and spoliation of every hunting-field. They dash off with the hounds the moment the fox is found, but happily the first fence stops them, and a fervent thankfulness is felt by every true lover of the chase as they pause discomfited, look dismally at the yawning chasm, and jog crestfallen away to the road.

There are many ladies, and estimable ladies, too, who take out their horses every hunting-day, and by keeping upon the roadways see all that they can of the hounds. Sometimes they are fortunate, sometimes not; it depends upon the line of country taken. Their position is, in my opinion, a most miserable one; yet they must derive enjoyment from it, else why do they come? They surely cannot imagine that they are participating in the hunt; yet it affords them amusement to keep pottering about, and enables them to make their little harmless boast to credulous friends of their "hunting days," and the "runs" they have seen throughout the season. Indeed, so far does this passion for boasting carry the fair sex, that I myself know two young ladies who never saw a hound in their lives, except from the inside of a shabby waggonette, yet who brag in so audacious a manner that they have been heard to declare to gentlemen at evening dances, "Really we cawn't dawnce; we are so tired! Out all day with the Wards--and had *such a clipping run!*"

This sort of thing only makes us smile when we hear it amongst ladies, but when men resort to it we become inspired with sufficient contempt to feel a longing desire to offer them severer chastisement than our derision.

I once asked a little mannikin, who had given himself the name and airs of a great rider, if he would be kind enough to pilot me over an intricate piece of country with which I was unacquainted. The creature pulled his little moustaches, and sniffed, and hemmed and hawed, and finally said, "Aw, I'm sure I should be delighted, but you see I ride *so deuced hard*, I should not expect a lady to be able to keep up with me." I said nothing, but acted as my own pilot, and took opportunity to watch my hard-riding friend during the course of the run. He positively never jumped a fence, but worked rampantly at locks of gates, and bribed country-folks to let him pass through. The last I saw of him he was whipping his horse over a narrow ditch, preparatory to scrambling it himself on foot.

And this man was only one of many, for the really accomplished rider never boasts.

PART III.

HUNTING.

CHAPTER VI.

HUNTING-GEAR.--NECESSARY REGARD FOR SAFE SHOEING.--DRIVE TO THE MEET.--SCENE ON ARRIVING.--A WORD WITH THE HUNTSMAN.--A GOOD PILOT.--THE COVERT SIDE.--DISAPPOINTMENT.--A LONG TROT.

Now that you are thoroughly at home on your saddle--in the park, on the road, and over the country--you are doubtless longing to display your prowess in the hunting-field, and thither we shall have much pleasure in accompanying you.

Your outfit will be the first thing to consider; and do not be alarmed when I tell you that it will require a little more generosity on the part of papa than you have hitherto called upon him to exercise.

To commence with your feet--which I know is contrary to custom--you will need two pairs of patent Wellington boots. These are three guineas per pair, but are a beautiful article, and will last a long time with care. Woollen stockings of light texture, with a pair of silk ones drawn over, are the most comfortable for winter wear. A small steel spur to affix to your left heel will be the next item required. The nicest kind are those with a strap attached, which crosses the instep, and buckles securely at the side. Of course, all ladies' spurs are spring ones, displaying no rowels which could tear the habit, but simply one steel projection with spring probe within, which, when pressed to the horse's side, acts most efficiently as an instigator. Latchford's patent is the best.

Two pairs of chamois riding-trousers, cloth from the hip down, and buttoning quite close at the ankle to allow of the boot going over, will be the next necessary; and you must also provide yourself with two riding corsets of superior shape and make.

Three habits of strong dark cloth, one of them thoroughly waterproof, will be required--the skirts to be made so short as barely to cover the foot, and so spare as to fit like glove, without fold or wrinkle. If a hunting-habit be properly cut it will require no shotting, which will be an advantage to your horse in diminishing the weight which he would otherwise have to carry. An elastic band nicely placed upon the inside in position to catch around the toe of the right foot will be sufficient to answer all purposes. You cannot do better, to procure an article such as I describe, than entrust your order to Wolmershausen (whom I believe I have already named in a former chapter), corner of Curzon Street, Mayfair, where you will not fail to find your instructions intelligently carried out. This firm has a speciality for skirt-cutting,--is, indeed, unapproachable in this particular branch, of what is in reality an ART; and even in these days of eager competition the old-established house suffers from no rivalry, and holds its own in the widely-contested field.

A very neatly-made waterproof jacket will be an addition to your wardrobe, as also a cape with an elastic band from the back to fasten around the waist, and hold the front ends securely down. This latter is an almost indispensable article. It is so light that it can be carried with ease in your saddle-strap, and in case of an unexpected shower can be adjusted in a single instant and without assistance, which is not the case with a jacket. It should be made with a collar, which can be arranged to stand up close around the neck, and thus prevent the possibility of damp or wet causing you cold or inconvenience. I approve of the jacket for decidedly wet days, when it should be donned on going out, but for a showery day the cape is preferable, as it can be much more easily taken off and again put on.

Two silk hats, with the addition of a melon-shape if you desire it--a long-lashed hunting-whip, and a plentiful supply of collars, cuffs, gloves, veils, and handkerchiefs, will complete your outfit. I, hunting four days a week, find the above quite sufficient, and if you care your things (having got them in the first instance of the best quality) it is surprising how long they may be made to serve. I have told you *how* to take care of them, but believe me, if you leave the task to servants the end will prove disappointing. You will never be one-half so well turned out, and your outlay will be continual.

It is an excellent precaution for a hunting-day, to look the previous morning at your horse's shoes; and do this yourself, for it not unfrequently happens that a careless groom will suffer him to go out with a loose shoe which gradually becomes looser, and finally drops off, perhaps in the middle of an exciting run, and obliges you to leave your place with the hounds and seek the nearest forge. All this sort of thing could, in nine cases out of ten, be obviated by a little care and forethought, but the majority of riders are too grand, or too careless, or too absurdly squeamish about the "propriety" of entering a stable, and not unfrequently too ignorant of things they ought to know, to see to such matters themselves, and so they are passed over and neglected. A groom is too often utterly careless. He is bound to send your horse from the yard looking shiny, and sleek, and clean. Any deviation from this would at once attract your attention, and arouse your displeasure. The groom knows this, and acts accordingly; but he also knows what you do not--that one of the shoes is three-parts loose; it will probably hold very well until you begin to go, and then it will drop off and leave you in a fix, perhaps miles away from a village where the damage could be repaired. The groom knew all about it, very likely, the day before, but he saw that you were not troubling yourself, and why should he? You never made any inquiry about such matters, nor seemed to interest yourself in them, and why should he be troubled concerning them? A loose shoe is nothing to him: it does not cause *him* any inconvenience, not it; then why worry himself? He does not want to bring the horse down to the forge through mud and rain, and stand there awaiting the smith's convenience; not a bit of it. He is much more comfortable lolling against the stable-door and smoking a pipe with Tom, Dick, or Harry.

It frequently occurs in the hunting-field that a horse loses a shoe in going through heavy ground, or in jumping a fence where he brings his hind feet too close upon the front ones, and, catching the toe of the hind shoe in the heel of the front, drags the latter forcibly off, and leaves it either on the ground behind him or carries it for a field or two hanging by one or two nails to his hoof, before it finally drops off.

The moment you are made aware that your horse has cast a shoe, which will generally be by somebody informing you of the fact, ascertain at once which of the animal's feet has been left unprotected. If the lost shoe happens to be a hinder one, the matter is less serious, but if a front one should be cast, do not lose any time in inquiring your road to the nearest smithy, and, whilst wending your way thither, be careful to keep as much as possible upon the grass by the roadside, that the shoeless foot may not become worn, nor suffer from concussion by coming in contact with the hard road.

It is a good plan to send your horse early to the meet: quite in the morning; or, should the distance be a long one, despatch him the previous evening in charge of a careful servant, and stable him for the night as near as possible to the point at which you may require him upon the following day. If you are fortunate enough to have a friend's house to send him to, so much the better a great deal; but under any circumstances it is pleasanter both for you and your animal that he should be fresh and lively from his stable, and not that you should get upon him when he is half-jaded and covered with mud, after a long and tiresome road journey.

To drive to the meet or go by train yourself is the most agreeable way. Some ladies ride hacks to covert, and then have their hunters to replace them, but this is tiresome, and not to be advocated for various reasons. If the morning is fine the drive will be pleasant, and you can then send your conveyance to whatever point you deem it most likely the hunt will leave off. You must, of course, exercise your judgment in the endeavour to decide this, but you may assist it considerably by asking the Master or the huntsman to be kind enough to give you a hint as to the direction in which they will most probably draw.

We will, then, surmise that you drive to the meet. It is an excellent plan, whether you drive or go by train, to take with you a small bag containing a change of clothing; leave this in charge of your servant, with directions where he is to meet you in the evening, and then, should you come to grief in a dyke or river you can console yourself with the knowledge that dry garments are awaiting you, and that you will not have to encounter the risk of cold and rheumatism by sitting in drenched habiliments in a train or vehicle. You will also, if wise, take with you a foot-pick and a few yards of strong twine. Even if you should not require them yourself you may be able to oblige others, which is always a pleasure to a right-minded and unselfish huntress. Take, likewise, a few shillings in your pocket to reward, if necessary, the wreckers, whose tasks are at all times difficult and laborious, and too often thankless.

Arrived at the meet, your horse and servant are waiting for you in good time and order; but it is a little early yet, and so you look about you.

What a pretty sight it is! How full of healthful interest and charming variety! The day is bright and breezy--a little bit cloudy, perhaps, but no sign of rain. A glorious hunting morning altogether. Numbers of vehicles are drawn up, filled with happy-looking occupants, mostly ladies and children. There are a good many dog-carts, polo-carts, and a few tandems, from which gentlemen in ulsters and long white saving-aprons are preparing to alight. It is nice to see their steeds, so beautifully groomed and turned out, led up to the trap-wheels for them to mount, without the risk of soiling their boots. Very particular are these gentlemen. The day is muddy, and they know they must be splashed and spattered as they ride to the covert-side, but they will not leave the meet with a speck upon horse or rider. There is a military-looking man--long, tawny moustache, and most perfect get-up--divesting himself of his apron, and frowning because his snow-white breeches are disfigured by just one speck of dirt; probably it would be unobservable to anybody but himself, yet he is not the less annoyed. A dapper little gentleman, in drab shorts and gaiters, is covertly combing his horse's mane; and a hoary old fox-hunter, who has just mounted, has drawn over close to the hedge, and extends first one foot and then the other for his servant to remove the blemishes which mounting has put upon his boots. This extreme fastidiousness is carried by some to an absurd excess. I remember upon one occasion seeing a gentleman actually re-enter his dog-cart and drive sulkily away from the meet because he considered himself too much splashed to join the cavalcade which was moving away to the covert, although he was fully aware that a trot of a few hundred yards upon the muddy road in company with numerous other horses would, under any circumstances, have speedily reduced him to the condition which he was then lamenting.

A few ladies come upon the scene, and many more gentlemen; and then comes the huntsman in proud charge of the beauties. The whips and second horsemen come also, and the Master drives up about the same time, and loses not a moment in mounting his hunter. The pack looks superb, and many are the glances and words of commendation which it receives.

Always have a smile and pleasant word for the huntsman and whips. They deserve it, and they value it. I always make it a point to have a little conversation with them before we leave the meet--in fact, I know many of the hounds in the various packs by name, and I love to notice them. Nothing pleases the huntsman more than to commend his charge: it makes him your friend at once. Many a time when I have been holding good place in a run, we have come across some dangerous fence which it would be death to ride in a crowd, and the huntsman's shout of "Let the lady first!" has secured me a safe jump, and a maintenance of my foremost position.

All being now ready, you mount your horse. It would be well if some gentleman friend or relative would look first to his girths, &c.; but, should such not be available, do not be above doing it yourself. Servants, even the best, are, as aforesaid, often careless, and a horse may be sent out with girths too loose, throat-lash too tight, runners out, or any of the thousand and one little deficiencies which an interested and careful eye will at once detect.

Of course you have not come to hunt without having secured a good pilot. You have, I hope, selected somebody who rides well and straight--boldly, and yet with judgment--for, believe me, a display of silly recklessness does not constitute good riding, however it may be thought to do so by ignorant or silly persons. Your pilot will ride a few yards in advance of you, and it will be your duty to keep him well in view, and not to get separated from him. This latter you may at times find difficult, as others may ride in between, but you must learn smartness, and be prepared for all emergencies. Moreover, if your pilot be a good one, he will see that you keep close to him, and, by glancing over his shoulder after clearing each obstacle, will satisfy himself that you also are safely over, and that no mischance has befallen you. Any man who will not take this trouble is unfit to pilot a lady, for whilst he is careering onward in all the glories of perfect safety, she may be down in some ugly dyke, perhaps ridden on, or otherwise hurt; and, therefore, it is his bounden duty to see that no evil befals her. I cannot say that I consider the position of a trusty pilot at all an enviable one, and few men care to occupy it in relation to a beginner or timorous rider, although they are ever anxious to place their services at the disposal of a lady who is known to "go straight."

In selecting a pilot, do so with judgment. Choose one who knows the country, and who will not be too selfish nor too grand to take care of you; for, remember, you are only a beginner, and will need to be taken care of. If, then, you have secured the right sort of man, and your own heart is in the right place, you may prepare to enjoy yourself, for a real good day's hunting is the keenest enjoyment in which man or woman can hope to participate in this life.

The trot to the covert-side is usually very pleasant. You and your horse are quite fresh. You meet and chat with your friends. The two, three, or four miles, as the case may be, seem to glide away very fast. Then comes the anxious moment when the beauties are thrown in, and all wait in eager suspense for the whimper which shall proclaim Reynard at home. But not a hound gives tongue this morning. You can see them--heads down, sterns up, beating here and there through the gorse--but, alas! in silence; and, after a while, someone says, "No fox here!" and presently your ear catches the sound of the huntsman's horn, and the hounds come trooping out, almost as disappointed as the field.

Then the master gives the order for the next or nearest covert, and there is a rush, and a move, and a long cavalcade forms upon the road, headed, of course, by the hounds. Get well in front, if you can, so as to be quite up when they reach their next try, for sometimes they find as soon as ever they are thrown in, and are far away over the country before the stragglers come up, and great, then, are the lamentations, for hunting a stern-chase is, to say the least of it, not cheerful. You will have another advantage, also, in being well forward, for your horse will get the benefit of a temporary rest, whilst those who, by lagging, have lost time at the start, are obliged to follow as best they can upon the track, bucketing their horses, and thus depriving them of the chance of catching their wind--which is, in a lengthened run, of very material consequence.

One especial difference you observe between road-riding and hunting: you are obliged to trot at a fast swinging pace such long tiresome distances from covert to covert, without pause or rest, and you feel already half tired out. Hitherto, when riding on the road, or in the park, if you felt fatigued you have only had to pull up and walk; but on hunting days there is no walking. The time is too precious, these short, dark, wintry days, to allow of such "sweet restings." The evening closes in so rapidly that we cannot afford to lose a moment of our time, and so we go along at a sweeping pace. Nobody who is unable to trot long distances without rest has any business hunting.

CHAPTER VII.

HOUNDS IN COVERT.--THE FIRST FENCE.--FOLLOW YOUR PILOT.--A RIVER-BATH. --A WISE PRECAUTION.--A LABEL ADVISABLE.--WALL AND WATER JUMPING. --ADVICE TO FALLEN RIDERS.--HOGGING.--MORE TAIL.

You have now arrived at the next covert, and have seen the hounds thrown in. In an instant there is a whimper, taken up presently by one and another, until the air rings with the joyous music of the entire pack, as they rattle their game about, endeavouring to force him to face the open. The whips are standing warily on the watch, the huntsman's cheery voice is heard encouraging the hounds, the Master is galloping from point to point, warning off idlers whose uninvited presence would be sure to send the "varmint" back into his lair. Your pilot, knowing that a run from here is a certainty, selects his vantage ground. Being a shrewd man, he knows that no fox will face a keen nor'-easter, nor will he be likely to brave the crowd of country bumpkins, who, despite the Master's entreaties, are clustering about yonder hedge. In short, there is only one point from which he *can* well break, and so your pilot prepares accordingly.

Another anxious moment ere the "Gone away! Tally-ho!" rings out upon the keen air; and then follows that glorious burst which is worth giving up a whole year of one's life to see. Hounds running breast high, fairly flying, in fact; huntsmen, whips, horsemen, all in magnificent flight, each riding hard for the foremost place, amid such a chorus of delicious music as is never heard from any save canine throats; and then, when the first big fence is reached, such hurry and scurry! such tumbling and picking up again! such scrambling of dogs and shouting of men! such cold baths for horses and riders! and oh, such glory amongst the wreckers, as they stand tantalizingly at the edge of the chasm in which so many are hopelessly struggling, whilst their audacious cries of "What'll you give me, sir?" "Pull you out for a sovereign, captain!" are heard and laughed at by the fortunate ones who are safe upon the other side.

Your pilot has been a wise man. He selected his starting-point at the sound of the very first opening out, and when the general scrimmage took place he had his line chosen, and so has led you wide of the ruck, yet in the wake of the hounds.

And here suffer me to advise you, if you should ever chance to be left without a leader, do not fall into the mistake of following the others, for my experience of hunting is that nine-tenths of those out do not know *where* they are going, nor where fox or hounds have gone before them. Cut out a line for yourself, and follow the pack. A pilot is, of course, a great acquisition, if he be a *good* one, but throughout some of my best runs I have performed the office for myself, and have succeeded in being in at the death. But then I am not a beginner, and I am surmising that *you* are. Keep about six yards behind your leader; follow him unswervingly, and jump after him, but not on him. Always wait till he is well out of the way before you take the fence in his wake. Your horse will jump more readily having the example of his before him, but I cannot too well impress upon you the necessity of allowing him to get well over before you attempt to follow. One of the ugliest falls I ever got in my life was through riding too close upon my leader. The run was a very hot one, and only four of us were going at the time. None, in fact, but those who had first-rate horses had been able to live through it. We came to a wide branch of a river, swollen by recent rains. My pilot, going a rare pace, jumped it safely; I came too fast upon him. My horse's nose struck his animal's quarters, which, of course, threw my gallant little mount off his balance, and prevented his landing. He staggered and fell back, and we both got a drowning! I was dragged up with a boat-hook, the horse swam on until he found a place to scramble up the bank, and then galloped off over the country. I recollect standing dismally by that river, my pilot and two wreckers scraping the mud from me, and wringing my drenched garments, whilst two or three more were scouring the adjacent lands in search of my truant steed. When, at length, he was caught, I had eleven miles to ride to the place at which I had left my trap, and was obliged on arriving to change every atom of my clothing, and wash off the superabundant mud in a horse-bucket, kindly lent for the occasion.

The fall involved the loss of the run, the loss of a habit, the loss of many odd shillings to wreckers, the loss of my temper, a wound from the boat-hook, and a heavy cold, the result of immersion on a perishing winter day. All these disasters were the punishments consequent upon my impetuosity in coming too close upon my leader; therefore, having thus myself suffered, I warn you, from woful experience, never to tread upon the horse jumping in advance of you. Allowing, even, that you do not cannon against him, there is another casualty which may not improbably occur. Supposing that he falls and throws his rider, your horse may in alighting just chance to plant a foot upon the empty saddle of the prostrate animal, the slippery nature of which throws him off his balance, and you and he roll upon the earth together--perhaps receiving a kick from your pilot's struggling mount. From this species of accident many evils have from time to time arisen, and therefore I dutifully endeavour to put you well upon your guard. I would also again remind you that if you really mean to ride an intricate country, you should never under any circumstances neglect to bring a change of clothing, for you may at any moment be dyked, and to remain in wet garments is highly dangerous,--not so long as you are exercising, but during the journey to your home. It is not in the saddle, but in vehicles and railway carriages that colds are contracted and the seeds of disease are sown. It may not be out of place here to offer you a piece of wholesome advice. Should you at any time have the ill-fortune to be riding a kicking horse in the midst of a crowd, always put back your hand when the cavalcade pauses, to warn those behind not to come too close to the heels of your unquiet steed. By so doing you may save an accident, and may, moreover, guard yourself from more than one anathema. I once saw the horse of a fiery old General kicked by the mount of a young nobleman, who thought it not worth his while to offer an apology. "See here, young man," said the irate officer, riding up to the offender's side, "whenever you come out to hunt on brutes like that you should paste a danger-card upon your back, and not run the risk of breaking valuable bones. I have said my say," he added, "and now *you may go to the devil!*"

A few hints next as to jumping.

If, in the course of a run, you meet with stone walls, do not ride too fast at them. Always steady your horse at such obstacles, and follow my oft-repeated advice of leaving him abundant head-room. If you have to cross a river or very wide ditch, come fast at it, in order that the impetus may swing you safely over; few horses can cross a wide jump without having what is called a "run at it." Never expect your animal to take such obstacles at a stand, or under the disadvantages consequent upon coming at them at a slow pace. Should the leap be a river or wide water-jump, suffer your horse to *stretch forward his head and neck* when coming up to it. If you fail to do so, you will most probably go in, for an animal who accomplishes his work requires his liberty as an absolute necessity, and, if denied it, will teach you, at the cost of a good wetting, to treat him next time with greater consideration. You will frequently see men ride pretty boldly up to some yawning chasm or ugly bullfinch--stop and look at it, hesitate an instant, and then, by cruel spurring, urge an exhausted animal to take it at a stand. This is truly bad horsemanship, and leads to many direful results. A good rider will, on perceiving that the obstacle is a formidable one, turn his horse round, take him some little distance from it, and then, again turning, come fast at it--quick gallop, hands down, horse's head held straight and well in hand, but without any pulling or nervous reining in. Such a one will be pretty sure to get safely over.

Should your horse, in jumping a fence, land badly, and slip his hind legs into a gripe or ditch, do not wait more than an instant to see if he can recover himself; you will know in that time whether he will be likely to do so. The best advice I can give you is to kick your foot free of the stirrup and jump off before he goes back. You will thus keep your own skin dry; and, if you have been fortunate enough to retain a light hold of the rein, you can rescue your horse without much difficulty; for an animal, when immersed, makes such intelligent efforts to release himself, that a very trifling assistance upon your part will enable him to struggle safely to your side, when you can remount him and try your chances of again picking up the hounds. Be cautious, however, in pulling him up, that you do so over smooth ground. I had a valuable young horse badly staked last season through being dragged up over a clump of brushwood after a fall into the Lara river.

Should your steed peck on landing over a fence you will be pretty certain to come over his head, for this is an ugly accident, and one very likely to occur over recently-scoured drains. You *may*, however, save both yourself and him, if you are *smart* in using your hands in assisting him to recover his lost equilibrium.

In the event of your horse jumping short with you, either from having taken off too soon or from any other cause, and falling upon you into a gripe, you may (when you gain a little experience) be able to stick to him without leaving the saddle. The first effort a fallen animal makes is to try to get up; therefore, if you are not quite thrown, hold on to his mane, and as he struggles to right himself make your effort to regain your seat. Be guided, however, in doing this by observing with a quick glance whether there are thorns or brambles overgrowing the place, for if there are, and your horse on recovering himself strides onward in the ditch, seeking a place at which he may get out, your face will undoubtedly suffer. This sort of thing once occurred to me in the course of a day's hunting. I held on to my animal when he fell, and regained my seat without very much difficulty, but before I could recover my hold of the bridle he had rushed forward, and my face was terribly punished by the overhanging brambles.

Be very careful, in this matter of holding on to a fallen animal, not to confound the mane with the rein. By clinging to the former you assist yourself without in the smallest degree impeding the movements of your horse; by clinging to the latter you seriously interfere with his efforts at recovery, and most probably pull him back upon you.

And this brings me to the subject of hogging horses' manes. Never, under any circumstances, allow an animal of yours to be thus maltreated. Not only is it a vile disfigurement, depriving the horse of Nature's loveliest ornament, but it also deprives the rider of a very chief means of support in case of accident. Many a bad fall have I been saved by clutching firmly at the mane, which an ignorant groom had oft implored me to sacrifice; and many a good man and true have I seen recover himself by a like action, when a hog-maned animal would undoubtedly have brought him to grief. Grooms are especially fond of this system of "hogging," and many a beauteous adjunct of Nature's forming has been ruthlessly sacrificed to their ceaseless importunities to be permitted to "smarten the baste." Tails, too, are remorselessly clocked by these gentlemen of the stable; not that they really think it an improvement, any more than they veritably admire the hogging process, but it saves them trouble, it lightens their labours, they have less combing and grooming to attend to. Tails were sent by Nature, not merely as an ornament, but to enable the animal to whisk away the flies, which in hot weather render its life a burthen. Man, the ruthless master, by a cruel process of cutting and searing, deprives his helpless slave of one of its most valued and most necessary possessions. I do not myself advocate long switch tails, which are rarely an ornament, being usually covered with mud; but I maintain that "docking" is cruel and unnecessary, keeping the hairs closely and evenly cut being quite sufficient for purposes of cleanliness, without in any way interfering with the flesh; therefore, do not reject my oft-repeated plea for "a little more tail."

CHAPTER VIII.

HOLDING ON TO A PROSTRATE HORSE.--IS IT WISE OR
OTHERWISE?--AN INDISCREET JUMP.--A DIFFICULT
FINISH.--THE DANGERS OF MARSHY
GROUNDS.--ENCOURAGE HUMANITY.--A RECLAIMED
CABBY!

To return to the subject of jumping.

In the event of an ordinary fall in landing over a fence, it is a
vexed question whether or not it is advisable to hold on by the
rein whilst your horse is on the ground. I do not now mean when
he is sunk in a ditch, but when he is prostrate upon even
grass-land or upon smooth earth. Many first-rate riders affirm
that it is a highly dangerous practice, therefore I am afraid to
advocate it, and must speak with reserve--as I did respecting the
management of a rearing animal--but for my own part I always
do it. My experience is, that when a horse struggles to his feet
his movement is almost invariably retrograde. He tries to get
away, consequently his heels are turned from me; and so long
as I keep my hold of the bridle his head will be nearest me and
his feet furthest. He will not think of turning to kick me, unless he
be a vilely vicious brute, not worth his keep; and so I can hold
him with safety until I am up myself and ready to remount him.
When my horse falls with me on the flat, I roll clear of him without
letting go the rein, and as the only danger of a kick is whilst he is
getting up, I shield my head with one arm and slip the rein to its
fullest length with the other, thus allowing the animal so much
head-room that he is enabled to make that retrograde
movement, or "dragging away," which is natural to him, and
which saves me from the possible contact of his heels.

This is, in my opinion (which I cannot, of course, pretend to think
infallible), the best course to pursue. It is the one which I always
adopt, and I have never yet, except in one trifling instance,

received a kick from a fallen horse.

I remember one day, a couple of seasons ago, I was riding hard against a very beautiful Imperial lady, who dearly loves a little bit of rivalry. Neck and neck we had jumped most of the fences for forty minutes or so, and both our steeds were pretty well beaten, for the running had been continuous, without a check. We came to an awful obstacle--a high thick-set hedge, so impenetrable that there was no chance of knowing what might be on the other side. There was but one little apology for a gap, and at this the Empress's pilot rode--immediately putting up his hand as a warning to us not to follow, and pointing lower down. I knew that when Bay Middleton thought there was danger, it did, indeed, exist; but I was too much excited to stop. We had the hunt all to ourselves, the hounds running right in front of us, and not a soul with them. I came at the fence with whip, spur, and a shout! My horse--than which a better never was saddled--rose to the leap, and landing upon his head after a terrific drop, rolled completely over. I was not much hurt, and whilst he was on his knees getting up, I scrambled back to the saddle, and went on; but, oh! under what dire disadvantages! My rein had caught upon a stake in the fence and was broken clean off, and I fancy it was this chuck to my animal's mouth which had thrown him out of his stride and caused him to blunder, for it was the first and last mistake he ever made with me, nor could I, in the hurry of regaining my seat unassisted, get my foot into the stirrup; so I finished the run as if by a miracle, and astonished myself even more than anybody else by bringing home the fox's brush as a trophy that I was in at the death.

Always bear in mind when hunting that you are bound to save your horse as much as possible. Jump no unnecessary fences; look out for a friendly gate whenever you can find one at hand; and in going up hill or over ploughed land, ease your animal and take your time. By acting thus judiciously you will be able to keep going when others are standing still. Always avoid bogs and heavy bottoms; they are most treacherous, and swamp many an unwary hunter in their dangerous depths. If you should ever have the bad fortune to be caught in one, dismount at once, and lead your horse. It is not a pleasant thing to have to do, but if you remain upon him, your weight, added to his own, will probably sink him up to his saddle-girths, and there he will stick.

I would desire particularly to impress upon you that if your horse carries you safely and brilliantly through one good run, you ought to be contented with that, and not attempt to ride him a second. It is through the unwise and cruel habit of riding beaten animals that half the serious accidents occur. Also remember that if you are waiting at a covert-side where there seems likely to be a delay, after your steed has had a gallop or a long trot, you should get off his back and shift your saddle an inch one way or the other, generally backwards, as servants are usually apt in the first instance to place the saddle too close upon the withers. By adopting this plan you will, when you again get upon him, find him a new animal. If you or I were carrying a heavy burthen upon our shoulders for a certain number of hours in precisely the same position, would it not make a new being of us to have it eased and shifted? And exactly so it is with the horse. A selfish man will sit all day upon his beast, rather than take the trouble of getting off his back; but against himself does it tell, for his animal is fagged and jaded when that of a merciful man is able to keep its place in the run.

There is nothing which should more fully engross the thoughts of the humane hunter than kindly consideration towards the noble and beautiful creature which God has sent to be the help of man. Your horse should be your companion, your friend, your loved and valued associate, but never your wronged and over-tasked slave. Humanity cries out with ready uproar against the long list of grievances which animals have to endure, yet how few of us exert ourselves to lighten the burthen by so much as one of our fingers! There is not one of us who may not, if he choose, be daily and hourly striving to curtail the load of misery which the equine race is called upon to bear. We may not be fortunate enough to possess horses ourselves upon which to exercise our humanity, but can we not do something--yea, much--for others? Surely we can, if we only possess the courage and the will. Even a word judiciously spoken will often effect more than we could have hoped or supposed. Two years ago I saw a cabman in Dublin cruelly ill-treating his horse. The poor animal was resting its worn and tired body upon the stand, ready for the wrench which its jaw would receive as soon as the next prospect of a "fare" should excite the cupidity of its owner. One would have thought that the sight of so much patient misery would have moved the stoniest heart to suffer the hapless creature to enjoy its few moments of needed repose. But no; the driver wanted some amusement, he was weary of standing by himself, without some sort of employment to divert his ignoble mind, and so he found such out. How? By beating upon the front legs and otherwise cruelly worrying with the whip the poor ill-used slave which he should have felt bound to protect. I saw it first from a distance--more fully as I came near--and with a heart bursting with sorrow and indignation, I crossed over and remonstrated with the man. I said very little; only what I have tried to inculcate in these pages--that humanity to quadrupeds is not only a duty which we owe to their Creator, but will in time repay ourselves. I expected nothing but abuse, and, indeed, the man's angry face and half-raised whip seemed to augur me no good; but, suddenly, as something that I said came home to him, his countenance softened, and, laying his hand quite gently upon the poor beaten side of the animal which he had been ill-treating, he said: "Well, if there was more like *you*, there 'ud be less like me! *that's* the thruth, at all events." And then he said no more, for he was satisfied that I knew I had not spoken in vain. For two years that man has been my constant driver. He is almost daily at my door: he drives me to and from the trains when going to and returning from the hunts, and dearly loves to hear something of the runs; nor is there a more humane driver nor a better cared horse in any city of the empire.

I have related this true incident, not from any egotism--God is my witness--but merely to show you how good is "a word in season." You may speak many which may be, or may seem to be, of none effect, but, like the "bread upon the waters," you know not when it may return unto you blessed.

CHAPTER IX.

SELFISHNESS IN THE FIELD.--FORDING A
RIVER.--SHIRKING A FENCE.-- OVER-RIDING THE
HOUNDS.--TREATMENT OF TIRED HUNTERS.--BIGWIG AND
THE MAJOR.--NAUGHTY BIGWIG.--HAPLESS MAJOR.

You must be particularly cautious in the hunting-field to avoid being cannoned against. There is no other place in the whole world where there is so little ceremony; and so very, very little politeness. It is verily a case of "Every man for himself, and the devil take the hindmost!" There is scarcely one man in the entire field who will not in his heart of hearts resent your presence, and so he will pay you no court. The crowding at gaps, and at certain negotiable places in different well-known fences is simply disgraceful; and persons--I cannot call them gentlemen--ride each other down like dogs. At such places you will be fortunate if you can enlist a friend to ride behind you, and thus prevent your being jumped upon in the event of a fall.

I must not omit to remind you that in crossing a ford your horse will be very apt to lose his footing. You will know when he does so by his making a kind of plunge, and an endeavour to swim, which he only does when he feels himself out of his depth. If at such a time you interfere with his mouth, he will *inevitably* roll over. Your only chance is to throw him the reins, and let him scramble or swim as he finds easiest. If the latter, lift your left leg (with foot still in the stirrup) completely over the third crutch, that he may not strike your heel with his near hind foot, or become in any way entangled with the stirrup or in your skirt. At the same time grasp the up-pommel firmly with your hand, that you may not be unseated when he makes his second struggle, which he will do as soon as he recovers his footing at the bottom of the water.

A horse who shirks his fences is a terrible infliction to have to ride. Of course the first refusal condemns you to lose your place, for it is the etiquette of the hunting-field that if your horse refuses you must at once draw aside and let the whole field go by before you again essay it. But, provoked though you may be, do not allow yourself to be vanquished. If you do not now gain the victory your horse will always be your conqueror. Bring him again to the leap, keeping his head straight and your hands low and firm. If he refuses a second time, bring him round again and again, always turning him from right to left--that is, with the pressure upon you right rein--and not suffering him to have his own way. Remember that if you suffer him to conquer you or bring him to any other part of the fence than that which he is refusing, you will thoroughly spoil him. Do not, however, treat him with harshness. Coax him and speak gently to him. It may be nervousness, not temper; and if so, you will soon get him over by kindly encouragement. The horse is essentially a timid creature. He is oftentimes subjected to cruelties for his "obstinacy," where a little kindness and a few reassuring words would be infinitely more effectual. Every glance of your eye, every look upon your countenance is noted by your horse whilst he can see you, and, when you are upon his back, your words fall upon highly sensitive ears. A horse's soul is full of affection for his owner. He *yearns* to please him. He would yield his life to serve him. Alas! how is such nobility requited? Man's cruelty converts a peerless and incomparable companion into a terrified and trembling slave. Young limbs are heavily weighted before they have had time to grow; dark, wretched, solitary confinement too early takes the place of the open air and free pasturage to which the creature would fain a little longer cling; young heads, pining for freedom, are tied or chained up in melancholy imprisonment. The numerous little devices with which the captive strives to while away the tedium of its captivity are punished as "vices" by heartless and ignorant grooms. Nervousness is called bad temper, and timidity regarded as a punishable offence. All the horrors of the modern stable are brought to bear upon the priceless creature who is born to freedom, and whose fettered limbs he is scarce permitted to stretch. A rack of dry, and oftentimes vitiated hay is placed *above* the head which was created to stoop to gather the juicy grasses of the earth. A measure of hard dry corn, or a bucket of water, is periodically brought and thrust before the prisoner, who eats and drinks for mere pastime, often without appetite, and whose frequent rejection of the offered dainties is regarded as "sulkiness" or "vice." The whole system of modern stable management is lamentably at fault. I cannot hope to remedy it. I cannot persuade obstinate humanity that the expenditure of a few shillings will turn in as many pounds: that by the bestowal of proper care, proper housing, light, and exercise, and proper clothing, food, and drink, the slave will repay by longer life and more active service the care and kindness which Christianity should deem a pleasure and privilege, instead of, as now, a compulsory and doled-out gift. I cannot expect to remedy these wide and universal evils, nor yet can you; but we are bound--you and I--to guard against such things in our own management. If your horse oppose you through nervousness, you can conquer him by kindness; if through obstinacy, which is occasional but not frequent, you must adopt a different plan. Use your spur and whip, and show that you will not be mastered, though you stay there till the stars come out. You will be sure to conquer ere long, unless your horse is one of those inveterate brutes which are, fortunately, rarely to be met with, and when you succeed in getting him over the obstacle at which he has sulked, put him at it again, making him take it backwards and forwards, and he will not be likely to trouble you by a repetition of his pranks.

You must be very cautious in the hunting-field not to leave yourself open to any suspicion of over-riding the hounds; keep close to them, but never so near as to be upon them. Over-riding hounds is a piece of unpardonable caddishness of which no gentleman, and certainly no lady, would be guilty; yet it is done; and then, when the master's wrath is aroused, the innocent suffer with the guilty, for many who are not absolutely offenders, ride too close in their zeal for the pleasures of the chase.

When your day's sport is over, and you are riding back to the place at which you expect to meet your trap, remember that the easiest way to bring your horse in is in a quiet jog-trot. It is nonsense to walk him, for he will only stiffen, and will be the longer away from his stable and his needed rest. If you chance to come across a piece of water, ride him to it and let him have a few "go downs,"--six or eight, but not more. When you get off his back, see that his girths are loosed at once, and, if very tired, a little water thrown over his feet. He should then be taken quietly home--if by road, in the same easy trot--and just washed over and turned into a loose box, where he can tumble and luxuriate without submitting to any of the worries of professional grooming. Fifteen minutes after my return from hunting, my horse--sheeted and comfortable--is feeding quietly in his stall, enjoying his food and rest; instead of standing in some wet corner of a cold yard, with his unhappy head tied up by an unsympathizing rope, and a fussy groom worrying his tired body with a noisy display of most unnecessary zeal. And this is as it ought to be. Horses are like human beings,--they like to *rest* when wearied, and their chief desire--if we would only believe it--is to be left alone. But we are incredulous, and so we hang about them, and fuss and worry the fagged and patient creatures who would fain appeal to us for a cessation of our attentions.

There are few things more truly delightful than a mutual understanding and affection between horse and rider, and this can easily be arrived at by kindness and care. I have a hunter--Bigwig, son of The Lawyer--who follows me all over the place, knows my voice from any distance, rubs his nose down my dress, puts it into my pocket to look for apples, and licks my hands and face like a dog; yet I have done nothing to induce all this, except treating him with uniform justice and kindness. He has carried me most brilliantly through three successive seasons without one single display of sulk or bad temper. He knows not the *touch* of a whip. I carry one, that the long lash, passed through his bridle, may assist him when necessary in getting over a trappy fence, at which I may deem it prudent to dismount, but the sight of it never inspires him with fear; if I showed it to him, he would probably lick it, and then gaze inquiringly at me to see if I were pleased with the novel performance. To me, this noble and beautiful creature is a priceless companion; yet, strange to say, nobody else (not even the most accomplished rider) can obtain any good of him. It is not that he displays vice, but he simply will not allow himself to be ridden. I once happened to mention this fact at our private dinner-table, in presence of a distinguished major, who had been boasting largely of his prowess in the saddle, and who at once offered to lay me ten to one that he would master the animal in question within five minutes. "I do not bet," I said, "but I will venture to assert that you will not be able to ride him out of the yard within as many hours." He took me up at once, and, as a good many sporting men were dining with us, who evidently enjoyed the prospect of a little excitement, I quietly called a servant, and sent orders to the groom to saddle Bigwig without delay. It was a lovely evening in summer, and we all adjourned to the yard to view the performance.

The moment my beautiful pet saw me he whinnied joyously and strove to approach me, but I dared not go near him, in case it should be thought that by any sort of "Freemasonry" I induced him to carry out my words. The sight was most amusing; the gentlemen all standing about, smoking and laughing; the horse suspicious, and not at ease, quietly held by the groom, whose face was in a grin of expectation, for none knew better than he what was likely to ensue. The major prepared to mount, and Bigwig stood with the utmost placidity; although I must confess he was naughty enough to cast back an eye, which augured no good to the gallant representative of Her Majesty's service. He mounted without difficulty, took up the reins, and evidently prepared for a struggle; but none such ensued. Bigwig tucked his tail very tight to his body, walked quietly forward for a yard or two, and then, suddenly standing up as straight as a whip, the defeated major slid over his tail upon the hard ground, whilst the horse trotted back to his box.

I have related for you this anecdote, not merely for your amusement, but to teach you never to boast. A braggart is ever the first to fall, and nobody sympathizes with him. If you become ever so successful in your management of horses, do not exert yourself to proclaim it. Suffer others to find it out if they will; but do not tell them of it, lest some day you share the fate of the prostrate and discomfited major.

CHAPTER X.

FEEDING HORSES.--FORAGE-BISCUITS.--IRISH
PEASANTRY.--A CUNNING IDIOT.--A CABIN SUPPER.--THE
ROGUISH MULE.--A DAY AT COURTOWN.-- PADDY'S
OPINION OF THE EMPRESS.

I said at the commencement of these pages that I should offer
little or no discourse upon the general management of horses;
yet, in one reserved instance, I may be permitted to break
through my rule. If you want your hunters to thrive, do not let
them have a single grain of raw oats. People have laughed at me
when I said this, and have scarcely waited for the turning of my
back to call me a mad woman; but a few of the scoffers have
since come to thank me, and if you adopt my plan you will think
that this little volume would have been cheap at a ten-pound
note. There are, of course, times when raw oats must be given,
for your horse may not always be in your own stable. At such
times it is a good plan to mix chopped clover or grass through
the feeding, taking care that grain and clover be thoroughly
mingled. The judicious mixture of green meat will go far towards
counteracting the binding effects which raw oats will be likely to
have upon a horse not accustomed to it, and will also induce him
to masticate his food, which an animal inured to softer feeding
will otherwise be apt to neglect, wasting the corn by dropping it
from his mouth in a slobbering fashion, making no use whatever
of his grinders, and swallowing a certain portion without chewing
it at all. I am, for various tried reasons, a thorough advocate for
Mayhew's and Shingler's style of feeding upon cooked food,
mingled, of course, with good sweet hay, or an admixture of the
juicy grasses upon which the animal in its unfettered state would
be prone to live.

In my stable-yard are a large boiler and an unlimited supply of
good water. The groom boils sufficient oats to do for two or three
days, and, when cool, mixes through it a small proportion of

bruised Indian corn. On this the horses are fed as with ordinary oats three times daily, and so enjoy the feeding that not one grain is left in the mangers, which are placed *low upon the ground*. The surest proof of the efficacy of this excellent and economical feeding is that my horses never sweat, never blow, never tire. When other hunters are standing still, mine have not turned a hair; and, as prize-winners and brilliant goers, they cannot be excelled.

The principle I go on is this:--If I eat a cupful of raw rice, it certainly does me no good; but if I boil it, it makes three or four times the quantity of good, wholesome, digestible food, every grain of which goes to the nourishment of my body. And it is precisely so with the oats and the horse. In addition to this feeding, I give abundance of good, sweet, *moist* hay, varied by green food in summer, substituting carrots in the winter-time, of which vegetable they are particularly fond. The carrots are given whole, either from my hand or put loosely in the manger. I never suffer them to be cut up, unless it be done *very finely*, either by myself or under my supervision, to induce a delicate feeder to taste his food through which the chopped carrots are rubbed. Grooms, with their accustomed ignorance, are almost always in favour of the "cutting up," but I regard it as a most dangerous practice. If the carrot be left whole the horse will nibble at it, and will bite off just such pieces as he knows he can chew and swallow, but there is more than one instance upon record of horses choking themselves with pieces of cut carrot, and very many who have nearly done so. I can feed my horses upon this system for very little more than half the sum which my neighbours are expending, with advantages which are certainly fourfold. I consider it an excellent plan to vary horses' feeding, as it tells quite as beneficially upon animals as upon ourselves;--and for this purpose there cannot, in my opinion, be anything better than the forage-biscuits, manufactured by Spratt & Co., Henry Street, London, ten of which are equal to one good feed of oats, and are so relished that not so much as a crumb is suffered to go to waste. They combine all the most nutritious of grains, with dates and linseed added in such proportions as experience has pointed out to the inventor to be the best. They are then baked, and thoroughly dried, so that they are entirely deprived of moisture, and will consequently keep good for any length of time. The baking process being complete, they are, when eaten, practically half-digested,--or, as I may say, they present the materials to the horse in the most digestible form in which it is possible to give them. There are certain chemicals used in very minute quantities in the manufacture of these biscuits, which are productive of highly beneficial effects upon animals thus fed,--improving their muscular development, and imparting to their coats a peculiarly healthy and brilliant appearance. One feed of the forage-biscuits three or four times weekly is the proper allowance,--and they should be given whole, as the same objection applies to the breaking of them as I have set forth in my dissertation upon the cutting up of carrots.

I now desire to warn you that if you hunt in Ireland you must be prepared for the laughable and most ingenious frauds which the poor people--alas! *how* poor--will certainly endeavour to practise upon you. I can, and do most fully, commiserate their poverty, but with their attempts at imposition I have long since lost patience. Doubtless they think that everybody who hunts is of necessity a rich person, and conceive the idea that by fleecing the wealthy they will aid in blotting out the poverty of the land. Nothing delights the old cottage-woman more than to kill an ancient hen or duck on a hunting-morning, and then, when the hunt comes sweeping past her door, out rushes the beldame with the bird concealed beneath her apron, and throwing it deftly--positively by a species of sleight of hand--beneath your horse's hoofs, kicks up a mighty whining, and declares that you have "kilt her beauty-ful fowl!" I was so taken aback upon the first of these occasions that I actually stopped and paid the price demanded; but, finding that the same thing occurred the following week in a different locality, I ascertained that it was a trick and declined to be farther hocussed.

It is likewise a common thing for a man to accost you, demanding a shilling, and declaring that it was he who pulled your ladyship's horse out of the ditch or quagmire on such and such a day. You do not remember ever having seen his face before; but if you are a hard-riding lady you will be so frequently assisted out of difficulties that you cannot undertake to say who nor how many may have helped you unrewarded, and, being unwilling that any should so suffer, you bestow the coin, most likely in many instances, until you find that your generosity has become known and is consequently being traded upon.

I remember one day, a couple of winters ago, when returning from hunting, I lost my way, and being desirous of speedily re-finding it, I accosted a ragged being whom I saw standing at a corner where four roads met, and inquired of him the most direct route to the point which I was desirous of reaching. The creature hitched his shoulders, scratched his collarless neck, pushed the hat from his sunburnt forehead, and, finally, looking down and rubbing the fore-finger of his right hand upon the palm of his left, thus delivered himself:

"I axed him for a ha'penny, and he wouldn't give it to me; but he put his hand into his pocket and pulled out a pinny, and gave it to me, and I took it in--ho, ho! and he gave me a letter to take up to Mrs. Johnston, and when I took it to her, she opened it and read it. Now, didn't I give her the letter?"

"Really," said I, "I know nothing about Mrs. Johnston nor her letter. I want to know the nearest way to Dunboyne station."

"I axed him for a ha'penny," began the man again. And then I had the whole story of the "pinny" and "Mrs. Johnston" repeated for me over and over, without a smile or any variation, until my vexation vanished, and I fairly roared with laughter. Guessing at once how the land lay, I produced a little coin with which I presented him, and which he immediately pocketed, and, touching his ragged feather, pointed down one of the roads, and said quite sensibly, "That's the right road, my lady." And so I found it. This man, I was subsequently informed, made quite a respectable maintenance by stationing himself at the cross-roads on daily duty, and informing every passer-by that he "axed for a ha'penny" but was generously treated to a "pinny," together with the story of Mrs. Johnston and her letter, accompanied by all the shruggings, and scratchings, and sniffings, which never failed to provoke the laughter of the hearer and to elicit the coveted coin.

The Irish, with all their little failings, are a hospitable people, and full of pungent wit. I was one evening wending my way to Sallins station, after a long and wearisome day's hunting. My tired horse was suffering from an over-reach, and I was taking him as quietly as I could, consistently with my anxiety to be in time to catch the train by which I desired to return to town. So utterly jaded were we both--I and my steed--that the way appeared very long indeed, and I asked the first countryman whom I met how far it was to Sallins. "Three miles," he told me, and I jogged on again. When we had traversed quite a long distance, and I thought I must be very near my journey's end, I ventured upon asking the same question of a farmer whom I met riding a big horse in an opposite direction to that in which I was myself going. It was a matter of about two miles, he told me, or mayhap three, but not more he thought, and I was certainly not going wrong; I was on the right road, and no mistake. I took out my watch. No hope for me now. I was undoubtedly late for the train which I had hoped to catch, and must wait two long hours for the next. A poor-looking little cottage was close at hand; to it I trotted, and looked in at the door. The family were at supper, all gathered about a narrow table, in the middle of which lay a pile of unpeeled potatoes and a little salt. The mule, upon which much of their fortune depended, was supping with them; thrusting his poor attenuated nose over the shoulders of the children, and occasionally snatching a potato, always receiving a box for so doing, to which, however, he paid no sort of heed. I was at once invited to enter, and gladly accepted the invitation, for I was cold and tired, pleased to ease my horse and get him a draught of meal and water. I sat down in the chimney-corner, thankful for the rest, but determined to withstand all entreaties to share the family supper, and my risible faculties were sorely put to the test, when my host, balancing a potato upon his fork and dipping it in the salt, presented it to me, saying, "Arrah! take it my lady, just *for the jig o' the thing*!" Of course I took it; and never have I enjoyed the richest luxury of an *à la Russe* dinner more than that simple potato in a poor man's cabin, in company with the mule and the pigs. When I stood up to go I carefully inquired the distance, for it was dark, and I had long since lost the remainder of my party. The man offered to accompany me to the station, and I believe he was actuated solely by civility, and not by any hope of gain. My horse was sadly done up; he had stiffened on the over-reach, and limped painfully. We proceeded but slowly, and, sighing for the patient suffering of my dearly-loved steed, I made the observation that the miles were very long indeed. "They *are* long, my lady," said the man, who was walking before me with a lanthorn; "but, shure and faith, if they're long they're narra'!" And with this most intelligent observation he closed his mouth, and left me to ponder upon it undisturbed until we arrived at the station.

One more anecdote, and I have done with them.

On one of last season's hunting-days the hounds met at Courtown, and great excitement was abroad, for the Imperial lady was expected to join the chase. She was, however, prevented through indisposition from attending, but Prince Liechtenstein and a very distinguished company came over from Summerhill. As we were trotting to the covert the country-folks were all on the alert, for not having heard of the disappointment respecting the Empress they were anxiously expecting her, and many were the surmises respecting her identity. I was riding close to the front, escorted by Lord Cloncurry, and as we swept past one of the wayside cottages, two men and a woman rushed out to stare at us and to give their opinions upon the "Impress." "Which is she?" cried the female, shading her eyes to have a good look,--"That must be *her* in front, with his lordship. Oh! isn't she lovely? A quane, every inch!"

"Arrah! shut up, woman," said one of the men, testily interrupting her. "That's not her at all, nor a taste like her! *The Impress is a good-lookin' woman.*" I need not say that this genuinely-uttered remark took the wind completely out of my sails, and that I have never since dreamed of comparing my personal appearance with that of any woman whom an Irishman would call "good-lookin'."

CHAPTER XI.

THE DOUBLE-RISE.--POINTING OUT THE RIGHT
FOOT.--THE FORCE OF HABIT. --VARIOUS KINDS OF
FAULT-FINDING.--MR. STURGESS' PICTURES.--AN ENGLISH
HARVEST-HOME.--A JEALOUS SHREW.--A SHY
BLACKSMITH.--HOW IRISHMEN GET PARTNERS AT A
DANCE.

I shall now touch very briefly upon one or two points which I have
not before mentioned, but which may, nevertheless, prove
interesting to some lady riders.

Firstly, then, I shall speak of the annoyance--sometimes a
serious one--which ladies experience from what is known as the
double rise in the trot. I have been asked is it preventible. Before
suggesting a remedy for anything--be it ailment or habit--we
must endeavour to get at the *cause* of the evil complained of.
The most successful medical men are those who first take time
and pains to ascertain the wherefore, and then seek to effect the
cure.

The extremely ungraceful and unpleasant motion known as the
"double rise" is attributable to two distinct causes. It is due either
to the horse or to the rider, and to the one quite as frequently as
to the other. A large, heavy animal, with slow and clumsy action
will, if ridden by a lady, be almost certain to necessitate the
double rise. This I know by the certainty derived from
experience. I was staying some time ago at a house in the midst
of our finest hunting county in Ireland, namely, royal Meath. The
owner was a great hunting-man in both senses of the word, for
he was a superb cross-country rider, and, if put in the scales,
would pull down sixteen stone. Being a top-weight he always
rode immense horses--elephants I used to call them, greatly to
his indignation. Very good he was about lending me one of these
huge creatures whenever I felt desirous of joining the chase,

which I confess was but seldom, for the first day upon which I accepted a mount we left off eighteen miles from home, and I was so exhausted by the time we arrived there, that I fairly fainted before reaching my own chamber. It was not the distance which tired me, although it was a pretty good one, but the fact that I was troubled with the double-rise all the way. I strove in vain to remedy it by urging my gigantic steed to a faster trot, and making him go up to his bridle; but the moment I began to experience a little relief, my companion--dear old man, now in heaven!--would say, "Well, that is the worst of ladies riding: they must always either creep in a walk, or bucket their horses along at an unnecessary pace. *Why* can't you jog on quietly, as I do?" He was clearly not suffering from the annoyance which was vexing and fatiguing me. I looked at him closely, watched his motion in the saddle--that slow, slow rise and fall--I compared it with mine, our pace being the same, and the mystery was at once solved. Both horses were trotting exactly together, keeping step, as the saying goes, yet my companion was at ease whilst I was in torment. Why was this? Because he had a leg at either side of his mount, his weight equally distributed, and an equal support upon both sides; in fact, he had, as all male riders have, the advantage of a *double* support in the rise; consequently, at the moment when his weight was removed from the saddle, it was thrown upon both feet, and this equal distribution enabled him to accomplish without fatigue that slow rise and fall which is so tiring to a lady, whose weight when she is out of the saddle is thrown entirely upon one delicate limb, thus inducing her to fall again as soon as possible, which, if riding a clumsy animal, she is constrained to do *at variance*, as it were, with his tedious and heavy motion, and hence the inconvenience of the double rise.

To illustrate my meaning, and explain more fully how it happens that men never complain of this particular evil: a man will be able to stand in his stirrups for a considerable time, even to ride a gallop so doing, because he transfers his weight *equally* to this feet; but how rarely do we see a lady balanced upon one leg!

Never, except it be for a single instant whilst arranging her skirt or trying her stirrup. The sensation is not agreeable, and would be, moreover, unpleasantly productive of wrung backs.

A heavy horse is never in any way suitable to a lady. It *looks* amiss. The trot is invariably laboured, and if the animal should chance to fall, he gives his rider what we know in the hunting-field as "a mighty crusher!" It is, indeed, a rare thing to meet a perfect "lady's horse." In all my wide experience I have met but two. Breeding is necessary for stability and speed--two things most essential to a hunter; but good *light* action is, for a roadster, positively indispensable, and a horse who does not possess it is a burden to his rider, and is, moreover, exceedingly unsafe, as he is apt to stumble at every rut and stone.

The double rise may also, as I said, be quite attributable to the rider. A careless way of riding may occasion it, sitting loosely in the saddle, and allowing your horse to go asleep over his work. Pull you mount together, so as to throw his weight upon his haunches, not upon his shoulders. Keep your reins close in hand. Rise, so that you shall be out of the saddle when his off fore-leg is thrown out, and I do not think you will have much to complain of from the annoyance occasioned by the double rise.

I have dwelt upon this subject because so many have asked me privately for a cure for it, and I have surmised that numerous others, who have not had opportunity--nor perhaps courage--to ask, will nevertheless be pleased to receive a hint.

It has also been inquired of me whether there is any remedy for that excessively unsightly practice of sticking out the right foot when in the saddle, as we have seen so many ladies do, until the toe is positively almost resting upon the horse's neck. There is, of course, a remedy; a most effectual one. *Don't do it.* It is quite possible and even easy to keep the right leg as close to the saddle as the left, the toe pointing downward, and the knee well bent. I know, however, that in some cases the position objected to is consequent upon the up-pommel of the saddle being placed too near the off one, thus there is not sufficient space for the leg to lie easily, and consequently it sticks out in the ungraceful manner so often seen and deplored.

In many instances, also, it is habit; a bad practice, indulged in at first without notice, and then, when confirmed, most difficult to eradicate. These pernicious habits are extremely apt to grow upon all of us, unless most carefully watched, I have seen ladies utterly disfigure their appearance in the saddle by placing a hand upon their side, or, worse again, behind their back, and riding along in this jaunty style with an air as though they thought themselves the most elegant creatures in creation. Others keep their elbows a-kimbo, and fairly churn themselves in the saddle with every rise and fall. Others, again, acquire a habit of tipping their horse with the whip in an altogether unnecessary manner. It is not actually enough to hurt the animal, but is amply sufficient to worry and ruffle his temper. No horse fit to carry a lady requires to be constantly reminded of his work. A whip in a woman's hand should be more for show, and to give completeness to the picture, than for purposes of castigation. Nothing looks worse nor more ungentle than to see it wantonly applied. It has been said, "Spare the rod and spoil the child," but I cannot agree with the theory. Rod and whip may be alike useful in (happily) isolated cases, but I do not envy the disposition of child or animal who cannot be made amenable by less ungentle means. Practices which are the result of habit may be checked, and quite effectually, by the bestowal of a little care. We want first some kindly friend to tell us of them; we next require the common sense and good feeling not to be offended at the telling; and, finally, we need the patience and perseverance which are born of the *determination* to overcome the fault. With regard to the telling, how few of us know how to tell! There are just the two ways, or perhaps I should say three. There is the cold, carping, disagreeable fault-finding manner, which picks holes for the mere pleasure of picking them, and the unworthy delight of seeing how the victim writhes beneath the torture. There is the snake-like, insidious fault-finding--the worst and most dangerous of all--which invariably commences with the words, "You know, my dear, I am only telling you for your own good." This species of fault-finding is peculiar to the *female* friend, and is invariably served up with an admixture of honey and gall, so skilfully compounded that the very soul of the listener is exercised and deceived. "Her words were smoother than oil, yet were they drawn swords." Lastly, there is the genuine, honest, open-hearted, fault-finding, which bears no malice, and is too true to clothe itself with the garment of deceit. By this alone we should be influenced or seek to influence others; but, for my own part, as I have already said, I have found the world so inordinately self-opinionated and determined *not* to be advised, that I have long since ceased to offer counsel, and only give it when requested. Long ago, when I first began to write, I was jealous of all interference, and invariably prefaced my letters to my Editors with, "Please do not alter anything in my MS." Poor blind child I was then, groping about in the dark, and sadly needing the helping hand which I was so obstinately rejecting. Well, we gain sense with years, and wisdom with experience. Now that I have got on in the world, in every sense of the word, I am only too anxious for advice, and ready to grasp at every friendly hint.

And so it should be with riding as with writing. Take all kindly counsel in good part, and if given advice ask for more. Bad habits grow upon us with giant force; they strengthen with our strength, because we know not of them, or blindly refuse to be controlled. I dare say a good many of us are acquainted with a very famous queen of song who always holds her hands crossed and her thumbs turned stiffly up whilst she is singing. I do not believe she is at all aware of the peculiarity of her attitude, and perhaps she could not sing half so well nor sweetly if she altered it. In like manner I told you, in the earlier portion of this volume, of a young lady who could not ride a yard without laying a firm grip upon the off-pommel of her saddle. These things are habit; we do them without consciousness; we are not aware of anything unusual in ourselves, but when the knowledge comes to us (which it soon will if we are known to possess sufficient sweetness to take a hint) we should turn it to advantage, and so improve with time.

I recollect that when these writings of mine were first issued in the journal to which they originally owed their appearance, a dear lady wrote to me all the way from Rhode Island, U.S.A., asking me for hints upon various subjects, and likewise offering me a few such, with so much sweetness that I not alone accepted, but welcomed and adopted them. She asked me many questions relative to the pictures with which my various subjects were illustrated, and admired very warmly the spirited drawings which Mr. Sturgess had made of my leap into the farmyard and also of "The first fence." Many of my readers may recollect them; and as there was, at the time, much discussion respecting the position of my feet as portrayed in the former picture, I take this opportunity of ranging myself upon the artist's side, for, after much thoughtful inspection of the picture, I arrived at the conclusion that he was perfectly correct, and the position quite such as must of necessity be, in the event of a runaway steed clearing such an obstacle with a wearied and startled rider scarce able to retain her seat upon his back. Even had the artist been mistaken--which I am bound to say he was not--the matter need scarcely have evoked criticism, for his strong point is his delineation of horses, and as he has no equal in this particular branch of art, he may well be forgiven if such trifles as a lady's feet occasionally puzzle him a little! Moreover, he draws with a view to producing effect as much as ensuring stereotyped correctness. I recollect when I saw that picture I sounded my protest against the flowing skirt and flying veil: two things quite foreign to my style of riding-dress, which is always severely close-fitting and *curtailed*. His answer certainly carried weight.

The skirt and veil were necessary to impart an appearance of rapid motion, or flying through the air. He was quite right, and I was decidedly wrong. I felt ashamed of myself, begged his pardon mentally, and atoned for my audacity by henceforward believing blindly in his judgment.

I recollect laughing much at the time at a grave suggestion made to me by a dear old lady, who thought there might be a particular reason why Mr. Sturgess was (in her opinion) less successful in depicting lady equestrians than when pursuing any other branch of his enchanting art. Neither she nor I had or have, unfortunately, the pleasure of his personal acquaintance, but we thought there might possibly be somebody in authority who strongly objected to his studying the details of the fair creatures whom he has occasionally to draw. To show that such things may be, and actually are, in real life, I recollect that when I was staying some two or three years ago at a famous house in the north of England, a gay harvest-home took place, and the servants and labourers had a dance in the barn. I and my husband, our host and hostess, and numerous guests staying at the castle, went out to see the fun, and greatly was I struck with the gallant appearance of the old barn, so gaily decorated with corn, and the fiddler fiddling away upon a beer-barrel! A mighty cheer was raised for us when we all, in full evening dress, joined the motley company of revellers, and the lord of the soil led off a country dance with a blushing mountain-lass, followed by her ladyship with an equally humble partner. The blacksmith was an Irishman, and looked very shy, as Irishmen invariably do in presence of the fair sex(?) I knew him as a workman upon the estate--I knew also that his wife, a very ugly woman, was a terribly jealous shrew--and, actuated by a spirit of mischief, I went and asked him to dance; but he only grinned, blushed, and said, "No, thank you, ma'am; *I'm a married man!*" My husband, who was standing by, said laughingly, "Why, Brian, you ought to feel flattered to be asked. Give Mrs. O'Donoghue your arm, and take your place for the dance." "O, faix," said Brian, hastening to obey, "if *you* have no objection, I'm sure *I* have none. *Let her come on!* Only," he added, pausing and scratching his head, "begorrah, *I hope my wife won't see me!*"

CHAPTER XII.

SUBJECT OF FEEDING RESUMED.--COOKED FOOD RECOMMENDED.--EFFECTS OF RAW OATS UPON "PLEADER."--SERVANTS' OBJECTIONS.--SNAFFLE-BRIDLE, AND BIT-AND-BRIDOON.--KINDNESS TO THE POOR.--AN UNSYMPATHETIC LADY.--AN UNGALLANT CAPTAIN.--WHAT IS A GENTLEMAN?--*AU REVOIR!*

My remarks upon the subject of feeding horses, having gained publicity through the columns of the press, have called forth much comment and adverse criticism. Some have evidently considered--and have not hesitated to say--that I have written the veriest twaddle; but happily there is a reverse side to the picture, and many (including one very august personage indeed) have expressed a determination to adopt my system. Beans are such excellent feeding that I cannot object to an admixture of them, and to most English horses they are almost a necessity; but in Ireland we care little about them. It is unwise to give too much hay. I said "abundance" on a former page, but the word, as I used it, did not signify a large quantity. For horses fed three times daily upon a plentiful measure of oats, crushed Indian corn, and beans if desired, a few handfuls of hay will be amply sufficient, and this should be placed where the horse can stoop to it, but never above him, as in the effort to disengage it from the rack the seeds fall in his eyes and produce irritation, and sometimes permanent disease.

A bran-mash on a Saturday night, or after a hard day, forms an admirable variety to the ordinary feeding routine. Let the bran be thoroughly well steeped and mixed, and a portion of cooked oats or chopped carrots intermingled with it. This will induce almost any animal to partake of the bran, from which otherwise many delicate feeders will resolutely turn.

I have strongly recommended cooked feeding, even against the uproar of a general outcry against it, because I have seen and proved its efficacy. Last November, on the first Tuesday in the month--the opening day with the Kildare hounds--we had a splendid run, during which, however, I was amazed to find that my great horse, Pleader, sweated heavily--a thing which had never previously been the case. In fact, it had always been my boast that when other horses were thoroughly done, mine had not turned a hair; but, on the day in question, he was in a white lather, and I thought appeared distressed. Upon coming home, and speaking about it in my stable, I was informed that the boiler was in some way out of order, and the horses had, unknown to me, been fed upon uncooked oats during the preceding three days. Had I required any confirmation of my theory, this circumstance would certainly have furnished it, and entirely defeats the general supposition that cooked food renders horses soft.

I have now given the best advice I can upon the subject of feeding, and I shall not again refer to it, nor to anything connected with the treatment or stable management of horses, as the subject is an endless one, everybody entertaining an opinion of his own, which it shall not be my ambition to upset. What I have said has been in kindness, and with a view to benefiting both man and beast; but I do not by any means expect the majority of my readers to coincide in my views. There is a stolid determination general throughout the world to stick to old customs and old-fashioned ways and habits, no matter how excellent the modern ones may be, and so the "horse and mill" go daily round. Masters object to my system because it involves an outlay in the erecting of a proper boiler and other necessary adjuncts; servants object to it because it gives them a little additional trouble. It is far easier to lounge to the oat-bin, fill a measure from it, and thrust it before the animal, not caring whether it is rejected or otherwise, than to fetch the water and fill the boiler and go through the labours of a process which, in itself exceedingly simple, is made to appear complicated and laborious by the amount of fuss and discontent which are brought to bear upon the work. There is an old saying, "If you want a thing well done, do it yourself"; but, unfortunately, there are some things--and this is one--which ladies and gentlemen cannot do, and there is no doubt whatever that servants accustomed to the old style of management will never willingly adopt the new--unless they belong to that rare and select and most exclusive *few* who have their masters' interest at heart.

Much information has been asked of me relative to the subject of holding reins. How often shall I say that there is no fixed rule, and that a method which may look well for park-riding will be totally out of place in the hunting-field. I have been asked how I hold my own bridle, and I shall answer that I almost invariably ride with a single rein, and you can understand my method readily if you will follow me whilst I endeavour to explain. Take your pocket-handkerchief, pass it through the back of any ordinary chair, and bring the ends evenly towards you, holding them for an instant with your right hand, which must, *pro tem.*, represent the buckle. Place your left hand within the loop thus formed, the little finger resting firmly against the near-side, about four inches above the right hand; grasp the opposite side between the forefinger and thumb, left hand (the two sides of the handkerchief representing the reins); press the off-side slightly inward with the pressure of your thumb, slipping it entirely away from the control of the right hand; then bring the near-side, which still is held loosely by the right, under the thumb of the left, and hold it firmly. You will thus see that you establish a sort of "cross rein," and that you have, and are able to maintain, a secure grip upon either side. By an outward movement or slight turning of the wrist, accompanied by pressure of the little finger, you will control your horse upon the near-side of his mouth, whilst by an inward movement and pressure of the forefinger you will be able to command him upon the other or off-side. It must be borne in mind that these movements should be from the wrist *only*, and not from the arm or shoulder. A good rider will keep the elbows close to the sides, just drawing the line finely between that pinioned look which is so disfiguring, and the detestable flapping, like the wings of an unquiet bird, in which so many riders, both male and female, so frequently indulge. I have seen ladies, who wished to have an appearance of hard riding, leaning forward in the saddle and working their elbows in an unsightly manner, the hands (influenced by the elbows) sawing also, and the poor horse, with open mouth and straining jaws, staggering along in distress, fighting his bridle, and presenting altogether a melancholy spectacle. A firm even seat, elbows close, head erect, and strong steady hands held *low*--these are the characteristics of a good and lady-like rider. In going across country put *both* hands to your bridle, and keep your horse's head straight and well in hand, but do not attempt to pull him nor interfere with him at his fences, or you will undoubtedly come to grief. If you ride with a bit and bridoon my advice is, ride your horse--even though he be a puller--upon the snaffle, and keep the curb rein looped over your little finger, hanging quite loose, yet in such a position that you can if necessary take it up at a second's notice.

I cannot too often impress upon you the advisability of being conciliatory and kind in your manner to everybody with whom you may come in contact. No matter how exalted your rank may be, you can all the better afford to be courteous to those beneath you. Kind words cost nothing, and are as balm to the hearer. Many of the lower orders are quite as much gentry at heart, and far more so, than those who hide their unworthiness beneath the convenient shadow of a "family tree." I have been more than once pained upon hunting days by the extreme contempt and rudeness with which ladies have treated the poor, who have asked nothing from them save the innocent and inexpensive privilege of seeing them mount and canter away with the field. It is all very well to say, "I do not like to be stared at," but even to those who *most* dislike it, surely it is worth a little self-sacrifice to see the undisguised enjoyment and listen to the original observations of the Irish peasantry, to whom a sight of the hounds--especially when followed by ladies--is a treat they never care to miss.

I was riding last winter in company with a lady, very noble, very handsome, very proud. We came up to a branch of a river, upon the brink of which some country folk had gathered, with the innocent desire of seeing it jumped. A poor man, very quiet-looking and harmless, was actually knocked down and immersed in the water by a reckless young officer, who galloped over him, and went on without even glancing back at the spot where the poor half-drowned creature stood wringing his dripping clothing, yet not uttering a syllable of reproach. My companion roared with laughter, first at the catastrophe, and then at me for sympathising with the sufferer. "Apologise!" she cried, in a high key. "*How* could Captain Dash apologise to a man like that? It would be different had he been a *gentleman*." I thought so too, if the meaning of the word "he" had only been reversed; but I said nothing, and we went on.

A few fields further we came to a terrible obstacle--a high post and rails, with a deep and yawning ditch upon the landing side. Three or four of us went at it: the rest turned away and sought the road. I got over safely, my noble Pleader proving himself, as usual, worthy of my confidence. Captain Dash came next, safely also; and then my ill-starred lady friend, whose horse (an inferior timber-jumper) bungled, and left her completely prostrate upon the wet earth. Never a pause did Captain Dash make in his onward career, although he glanced back when he heard her shriek, and, incredible as it may appear, I thought I saw him smile, for it was ever his saying that ladies had no business hunting, and always deserved mischance; but the poor man, at whose immersion she had laughed a few moments before, came running to her relief, rendered her every assistance in his power, replaced her in the saddle, expressed regret for her accident, and positively declined to accept of any remuneration for his services.

Which of these men, think you, was the gentleman? I know what I thought respecting the question; and I judged that my friend's opinion was formed as mine, for she now loves and cares the poor, and suffers the rich to care themselves, as every true-hearted and Christian woman should; and, moreover, on glancing over a book of my poems which I lent her some time later, I found a leaf turned down, as though to mark these lines--

"What is a gentleman? Is it a thing Decked with a scarf-pin, a chain, and a ring, Dressed in a suit of immaculate style, Sporting an eye-glass, a lisp, and a smile? Talking of operas, concerts, and balls, Evening assemblies, and afternoon calls, Sunning himself at "at homes" and bazaars, Whistling mazurkas, and smoking cigars?

"What is a gentleman? Say, is it one Boasting of conquests and deeds he has done, One who unblushingly glories to speak Things which should call up a flush to his cheek? One who, whilst railing at actions unjust, Robs some young heart of its pureness and trust; Scorns to steal money, or jewels, or wealth, Thinks it no crime to take honour by stealth?

"What is a gentleman? Is it not one Knowing instinctively what he should shun, Speaking no word that could injure or pain, Spreading no scandal and deep'ning no stain? One who knows how to put each at his ease, Striving instinctively always to please; One who can tell by a glance at your cheek When to be silent, and when he should speak?

"What is a gentleman? Is it not one Honestly eating the bread he has won, Living in uprightness, fearing his God, Leaving no stain on the path he has trod? Caring not whether his coat may be old, Prizing sincerity far above gold, Recking not whether his hand may be hard, Stretching it boldly to grasp its reward?

"What is a gentleman? Say, is it birth Makes a man noble, or adds to his worth? Is there a family-tree to be had Shady enough to conceal what is bad? Seek out the man who has God for his Guide, Nothing to blush for, and nothing to hide; Be he a noble, or be he in trade, *This* is the Gentleman NATURE has made."

Now, kind reader, farewell. If I have given you instruction, called a laugh to your lips, or taught you to prize and cherish the priceless creature which God has generously sent for our enjoyment and our use, I shall cheerfully lay aside my pen, happy in the conviction that I have not written in vain.

Yet, shall I say in the song-words,

"*Au revoir. Pas adieu!*"

for we meet again, I trust, soon and often; but the subject upon which I have been writing has come to an end.

Whilst acknowledging the kindness of my friends, I would desire also to shake hands with my enemies. Life is short, and so it behoves us to bear no malice. To those who have unkindly criticised me I offer freely a forgiving hand and heart. I have never wilfully offended any, and if my efforts have not come quite up to the standard of excellence which certain captious critics have set up, I have at least done my best, and have been careful, in propounding theories which might appear new and uncommon, to state that such things were according to my notions, in which, however, I did not expect all persons to coincide. So long as the world lasts so long will there be differences of opinion; but it is not because such exist that ill-feeling should creep in, and Christian charity become a thing of nought. In ancient days, when the Apostles were upon the earth, these things were as they are now; yet the Great Example, to whose pure and simple teaching we all hopefully look, inspired the command, "*Let brotherly love continue.*"

So be it, reader, with you and with me.

PART IV.

HUNTING IN IRELAND.

There is at present a mighty outcry in our poor land. Not against "battle, murder, and sudden death," landlord-killing, and "Boycotting," but against our royal pastime--hunting. The tenant-farmers are uproarious in their opposition to it; and, with a headstrong determination which cannot be too strongly condemned, refuse to listen to the voice of the reasoner. We are but in the beginning of our season, yet is our prospect marred and our pleasure spoilt by the blind idiotcy, not of the few, but, unfortunately, of the many.

They have but one cry, "You are ruining our grass-lands!" A more egregious error could not possibly exist. Is it wilful blindness or merely the desire to banish landlordism from the country which induces this senseless outcry? If the latter, there is unhappily every probability that the outcriers will succeed; if the former, there may be some hope of ultimately unclosing their sealed eyelids.

A body of horsemen galloping over grassland during the hunting season can never occasion injury; it is simply an absurdity to endeavour to maintain a contrary theory. A great friend of mine and a most practical gentleman, who possesses a large common attached to his grounds, upon which he can, if desirable, exercise his horses, always prefers doing so throughout the winter upon his finest grass-land. He maintains, and correctly, that they do it an immensity of good, and once offered (to prove the correctness of his judgment) to give the use of the said land to the colonel of a cavalry regiment stationed in his vicinity--to do all his work upon throughout the winter months. The offer, after some demur, was accepted, and proved to be most advantageous to the land-owner.

Being an enthusiastic follower of the Ward Union stag-hounds, I am enabled to state that I have galloped with them, in company with at least two hundred other riders, across the Ward Country and over the Fairyhouse lands, which are--as is well known--of a singularly wet and holding nature; and this not once, but many times throughout the season. Yet, so early as April, at which date the famous Fairyhouse races take place, no track or footmark can be seen upon the luxuriant grass. Again, when riding in winter through Phoenix Park, I have been struck by the state of mud to which it has been reduced through the frequent galloping of horses over its surface; yet, in summer it grows the finest grass, and is as smooth as a billiard-table. One day in June, three years ago, a grand Review was held there in honour of the Queen's birthday. A terrible shower came down--one of those mighty floods which can, in a few moments, transform a beauteous green sward into a hideous mass of unsightly mire and dirt. Those on foot ploughed patiently through it, sinking ankle-deep at every step; those upon horseback, myself included, churned it beneath their horses' feet, until not a trace was visible of the emerald carpet, which, one short hour before, had afforded firm footing for many thousands of spectators. Three weeks later, I rode through that park again; the velvety turf was green and fresh as ever, nor was there visible *one trace* of the countless feet which had, as it were, waded over it so short a time before. The day upon which St. Stephen's Park was, through the princely generosity of Lord Ardilaun, opened to the public, was a wet, or at least a damp one, and thousands upon thousands of roughly-shod feet cut up the grassy sward; yet, in a few brief days, it was rich and verdant as before. Nor do I think there is in our noble Phoenix Park a more luxuriant stretch of grass-land than is "the nine acres" upon which polo players continually assemble.

Having thus, then, endeavoured to prove that the galloping of horses is in no way injurious to pasture lands, I shall proceed to the consideration of other matters connected with the subject in question.

If hunting in Ireland were abolished, then indeed might the cries of her children ascend heavenward, for I know not what would become of her! The gentry who are now resident landlords, maintaining large and costly establishments, would migrate to other countries and more genial climes. Servants would seek in vain for employment. Boot-makers, clothiers, saddlers, harness-makers, would find no custom. The farmer would sigh vainly for a price for his corn. Hay and straw would be a drug in the market. Hunting-lodges would remain unlet, growing mouldy with time and damp. Butchers, bakers, poulterers, butter-makers would be alike involved in one common ruin; for the houses of the gentry would be empty, and desolation would overspread the land! No buyers then for high-priced hunters and promising colts, which now command so high a figure; no merging of grades and mingling of classes in that happy contact which the hunting-field so well engenders; none of that delicious feeling of equality which the peer and the peasant seem alike to acknowledge whilst participating side by side in the dangers and excitement of the chase. All would be stillness, solitude, and gloom!

Suffer me, then, to implore my countrymen and countrywomen to do all in their power to promote the pleasures of hunting. It must immensely benefit even those who do not actually participate in the sport, inasmuch as it brings rich and poor into happy contact, and causes a vast amount of money to be circulated, which enriches the pockets of the poorer classes, and brings grist to many a mill which would otherwise stand desolate, with disused and motionless wheel. To us who *do* participate in it, there is no need for speech. Which of us does not know the pleasures of preparing for the glorious sport? the early rousing up from slothful slumber, the anxious outward glance at the weather, that fitful tyrant which makes or mars our enjoyment; the donning of hunting garments, the packing of sandwich boxes, the filling of flasks with whisky, or better, *far* better, with strong cold tea; the cheery drive to the meet, the many happy faces assembled there, the greetings amongst friends, the praisings of the pack, the trot to the covert, the dashing of the hounds into the gorse, the sweet music which proclaims that Reynard is at home, the joyous sound of the "Gone away!" the hurry-scurry to be first and foremost in their wake, the anathemas hurled against those who are over-riding them, the tumbling at the fences, the picking up again, the drowning in the rivers, the fishing out by the wreckers, the maddening excitement of traversing an intricate country, the wild desire to be in at the death, the saving of our horses over holding lands, the riding of them up to their bridles where the going is good, the last mighty effort, the final fence cleared, and the canter up to where the huntsman is holding aloft the brush and mask, and the hounds are breaking up their fox! Who that has ever experienced these joys will be likely to forget them, or will fail to promote, by every means in his power, so health-giving and enlivening a sport?

We have one very serious drawback to our hunting in Ireland, and, indeed, in many other places also--namely, wire fencing. I saw something of a tragic incident occur last season whilst hunting with the Meath hounds. We came up to an impassable fence, and all made for the gate, which was open; but the owner of the land rushed out from his dwelling, shut it in our faces, and insolently refused to allow us to pass. Threats and entreaties were alike vain. He called us every name in the calendar, and consigned us all to a very ugly place, in language which was certainly not parliamentary. Many of the field turned off and sought another way, but two or three of the bold ones charged the gate, and got over, clearing man and all! I and one other took the fence--a mad proceeding, which gave us both an ugly fall;

but we scrambled up somehow, and succeeded in picking up the hounds. Late in the evening, whilst hunting another fox, he led us over the same identical ground, and a hard-riding gentleman, first at this mighty obstacle, charged it boldly, but, alas, with what a result! The farmer had, during our absence, run a stiff wire through the fence, which, catching the horse in the breast, turned him completely over, breaking the rider's arm, and otherwise severely injuring him. Some members of the hunt, seeing what had occurred, besieged the offender's dwelling, and he had an extremely uncomfortable ten minutes. I have heard persons aver that the man was badly treated, and that he had a perfect right to wire his fences if he so willed. Undoubtedly he had, if it were done openly and in such a way that the wiring could be discerned, but not, by petty treachery, to imperil the safety, if not the lives, of a large number of persons.

My advice to farmers would be this; wire the fences if necessary; but, at the commencement of the hunting season, cut away, say twenty yards of the wiring at the poorest point of the field, and mark the spot with a pole and flag. Every rider would assuredly make for it as being the only jumpable place, and at the close of the season a few boys with five-grained forks would speedily set all to rights; nor can there be any doubt that the best crop in the field would be on that particular spot. Allowing even for a moment, for argument's sake, that expense, trouble, or loss might be thus occasioned, there is not a master of hounds in all Ireland--neither, I fancy, in any other country--who would not willingly and cheerfully indemnify the owner of the land. But so long as the world lasts, so long will there be blindness; and until the "happy hunting-grounds" are reached, horses and horsemen will be daily anathematised by the self-willed cultivators of our native soil.

PART V.

HUNTING IN AMERICA.

There is a great land across the Atlantic where they do great things, and utter great sayings, and patent great inventions, and erect great buildings--and where, in short, the inhabitants beat us (as they themselves say) "all to fits!"

A mighty nation they are, too--God prosper them as they deserve; but there is one thing at least in which we can say, without boasting, we are able to beat them, and that is, in our hunting. A fox-hunt in America is a very tame and inglorious proceeding, and one which decidedly would not come under our definition of "sport."

American hunting differs in the first instance from ours, inasmuch as it is always a summer pastime. The extreme severity of the winters necessitates this, as during the cold season neither men nor horses can work.

The disadvantages of summer hunting are of course numerous. The heat is excessive, and the crops are in the ground. Most of the American farmers and graziers own their land, and the greater number of them will not suffer hoofs to cross it. This is partly from a spirit of surly independence--partly from an ignorant determination to hold with stolid obstinacy to that most erroneous belief, that the galloping of horses is injurious to grass-lands. But, anyhow, the objection exists; and as it is vain to attempt to overrule it, a compromise is effected between hunting under difficulties and not hunting at all.

The system pursued is this. A man--usually a stout-limbed peasant--is sent out, who drags an aniseeded bag across country, and over the lands and fences of such as will permit it, or who are themselves in the habit of joining in the chase. Then, when the field has assembled, the hounds are laid on, and work their way after the drag, a "bag-man" being provided to blood them at the finish. Sometimes the pack comes too close upon the dragger, and then a nasty scene ensues, which is pleasanter not described.

Fortunately for men, horses, and hounds, hunting is but little indulged in throughout America. I mean, of course, fox-hunting, for I cannot attempt to cry down the many splendid and manly hunts of other descriptions in which the Americans carry off the palm.

In many parts of the country--more especially in the States--the people so affect trotting-horses, that the matter has become a craze. It is a fact, which has more than once been proved, that four legs capable of carrying any sort of frame a mile in less than two-and-a-quarter minutes, will easily fetch a thousand pounds; and if the animal is in condition to repeat the performance several times in one day, his price will range correspondingly higher.

The usual arrangement--very seldom varied--is that the "trots" shall be mile heats; and as the horses are, generally speaking, pretty well done up at the finish, owing to pace, excitement, and temperature, twenty minutes are allowed between each heat for "cooling off" purposes.

When a horse is distanced in one of these trials, he is at once withdrawn; and the judges have the privilege, which they use, of distancing a horse for breaking--or, as we would say, commencing to run--which is, as may be supposed, a thing most difficult to prevent.

Sometimes a racehorse is hitched double with a trotter. This is called, in American parlance, a running-mate. The runner takes all the weight and draft of the "sulky," and the trotter merely trots alongside of him. It requires a very level-headed horse to keep evenly to his trot, with a runner tearing away at sweeping pace beside him, and the trial is regarded as simply one of skill, and is rarely successful. A trotter who can coolly and evenly maintain his trot when hitched with a racer, can command for his owner any amount of money, even though he be in all other respects comparatively worthless.

Races, of which many are held at Rhode Island, are as distinct as possible from trots. The courses are made circular; as much so, at least, as the lie of the land will permit, and are beautifully constructed, the grading being especially attended to. They are generally enclosed by a very high boarded fence, an admission fee being charged at the opening. This arrangement is found to answer admirably, as the amount demanded--although not an extravagant one--is sufficient to exclude a goodly number of racing roughs, whose interest in the sport is not more keen than their desire to investigate the contents of their neighbours' pockets.

Trotting-tracks are constructed upon the same principles as race-courses, but the track is harder. Sometimes, however, although not frequently, races and trots are held over the same course, and when this is done the track is carefully softened for the races, by a harrowing process, which is most carefully carried out.

Most of the hacks and hunters in use in America--a very large portion, at least, of the saddle-horses--are racers which have been rejected from the racing-stables. This is particularly the case at East Greenwich, and throughout the States. Some of these horses are "weeds," but a few of them are well worthy of the high prices given for them, being really splendid animals, in spite of the crabbing which they receive at the judge's hands before they are thrown out of the contest, and passed over to the proprietorship of dealers in hacks.

Very fine horses of the hunter class are bred in Kentucky--the Yorkshire of America--and are sold at comparatively low rates. I saw a magnificent chestnut, seventeen two in height, with grand action, and so superbly ribbed-up and built as to be capable of carrying twenty stone, which had been sold there to an enterprising Irish speculator for three hundred and twenty dollars, a good deal less than eighty pounds of our money. The animal afterwards fetched upwards of six hundred guineas at Tattersall's, to carry a top-weight millionaire with the Whaddon Chase hounds. This was, however, an exceptional case, for it is not usually an easy thing, nor even possible, to make money by trading in Kentucky hunters. A few speculative European dealers have from time to time tried it, but their efforts have not been crowned with the anticipated reward, the reason being, that travelling expenses swallow up profits. Seven days and nights of constant journeying must be gone through before the animals are brought to the Atlantic sea-board; and then there is the crossing to encounter, with its cost and perils. Altogether, it is scarcely a profitable venture, and some who have embarked in it will, I know, be quite ready to endorse my opinions upon the subject.

Stag-hunting used to be very prevalent in distant parts of America. Strangers traversing tracts of country north of the Ohio will be told this by guides and fellow-travellers, and will marvel that in such a district it could ever have been a popular sport. Anything more perilous it would be impossible to conceive, the "going" being principally up and down precipitous inclines, dotted at frequent intervals with huge boulders, half buried in the reedy grass, over which the horses blunder and stumble at almost every stride,--not unfrequently hurling their riders headlong down some dangerous ravine.

Those who have enjoyed the very doubtful pleasure of hunting at the Cape, know something of the perils of the Mimosa tree, which grows there in such deadly luxuriance. A similar danger-trap exists in the stag-hunting districts of America, the long sharp thorns proving terribly destructive to the flesh of man and beast.

It is almost impossible to escape these trees. They grow singly and in groups, with long, light, swaying branches, treacherously outstretched; and if an excited steed, or an unwary rider comes too near to one of them, no close-set company of razors could do more cruel injury, nor make greater havoc of saddlery and clothing.

When we come to regard the question of district hunting in a comparative light, few will hesitate to admit that in spite of all the drawbacks consequent upon wire-fencing, fox-trapping, and hound-poisoning, there are worse countries to hunt in than dear old England; and we who know the sweet delights of a good gallop over rich grass-lands, dotted picturesquely with the harmless beech or elm, and with nothing more dangerous to negotiate than fair broad fences and five-barred gates, need never sigh for the yawning ravines of foreign hunting-grounds, with their treacherous boulders and dangerous Mimosas.

CORRESPONDENCE.

LADIES ON HORSEBACK.

To the Editor of *The Illustrated Sporting and Dramatic News.*

SIR,--I have read with keen interest the article on "Ladies on Horseback" in your last number. I find several things in it which differ from my preconceived ideas, but it is impossible not to perceive that the writer, Mrs. Power O'Donoghue, speaks from an experience which makes her an undoubted authority. With reference to safety-stirrups, for instance. I have always seen that the ladies of my family were provided with them, and your contributor's objection seems not to be based upon the mechanism of the stirrup when in proper order, but on the circumstance that it is "almost invariably stiff," through neglect. I must admit that I have seen a lady hung up in a safety-stirrup; but surely it is possible to see that the stirrup will work before setting out for a ride or a day's hunting, and if the iron is large enough, so that "the padding over the instep" will not "cause the foot to become firmly embedded," are we to understand that the safety-stirrup is objectionable? Mrs. Power O'Donoghue has a poor opinion of "John the coachman, and Jem the groom," but I am lucky in having trustworthy people in my stable. What stirrup would your contributor have instead of the one with which so large a proportion of ladies ride? Another thing that I should like to know more about is the saddle recommended in the article. "Accustom yourself from the beginning to the use of a properly constructed saddle, made as straight as a board, no dip whatever," this writer says. Now I have never, so far as my recollection goes, even seen such a saddle, and may I ask what are the advantages of a thoroughly straight saddle, and what are the disadvantages of the inevitable slope or dip? I ask purely for information, for I am perfectly ready to submit my judgment and hitherto received notions to the dictum of a lady who is clearly so competent to treat the matter as your contributor. Would the lady have straight saddles also for men? is a question which incidentally occurs to me. I am far from supposing that a thing must be right because it is in general use, but there seem good reasons for the adoption of the ordinary shaped saddle, and I should be very glad if your contributor would let us know her reasons for departing from custom.

Before concluding, let me thank you for a series of articles which cannot fail to be of value to those for whom they are intended.

I am, Sir,

Your obedient servant,

H. DE V. R.

* * * * *

SIR,--I feel bound to answer the letter of "H. de V. R." which appeared in your journal of last week's issue. With regard to the "safety-stirrup," there could not be much objection to it if it were made sufficiently large to prevent the padding over the instep from causing the foot to become embedded; and if, likewise, some careful and competent person were ready and willing to give the machinery of it a thorough examination immediately before entrusting the safety of a lady to such an uncertain support. But how seldom is this the case? Servants--even the most careful--are, to say the least of it, apt to overlook these important details; and when the steed is led to the door the cavalier who is to escort the lady is too much occupied in admiring his fair charge, talking to her, arranging with her where they shall ride, fastening her gloves, or performing a like office for himself, to worry his head about such an apparently insignificant thing as her stirrup. Provided he ascertains that it is the required length, he troubles himself no further about it, and probably in nine cases out of ten the dandy youth would not even comprehend the meaning of the term "safety" as applied to the article in question. No doubt it often happens that an elderly father, a matter-of-fact husband, a phlegmatic uncle, or a careful brother may be upon the spot, with wits and hands ready to avert danger; but how frequently, also, is it the fashionable stripling who escorts the lady--a cousin, or a lover, perhaps--ignorant of all connected with riding, except the pleasure of it; or the booted and belted servant, who touches his hat, and thinks he has done his duty because the saddle is clean and the horse sleek and shiny; or the riding-master, who has come out in a hurry, anxious and flurried at the last moment to see that everything *looks* right, and who has had no time to see after such minor accessories as stirrups, or has left the matter (if he thought of it at all) in the hands of the groom, who has left it alone altogether. This being the case, I maintain that a stirrup encumbered with machinery is unsuited to a lady, because, although she may have an escort who will look after it, there is the possibility that she may not have such good fortune. Moreover, a stirrup made sufficiently large to bear padding over the instep, and yet enable the foot to slip easily in and out, must of necessity be a considerable weight, and this alone would be an objection, especially to a hunting lady, who calculates to a nicety every ounce which her steed has to carry. I have said that a small racing, or jockey-stirrup, is the *nicest* in which a lady can ride, and I am bound to adhere to my judgment.

So much for the first portion of "H. de V. R.'s" letter. Now we come to the second.

My "poor opinion of John, the coachman, and Jem, the groom," is based, not upon their untrustworthiness, but upon their want of capacity as teachers of the equine art. I have never yet, in all my experience, met with any servant who was capable of instructing a lady how to ride; yet I have been fairly astonished to find the contrary idea quite general amongst parents in the country, who fondly hope that their daughters may one day adorn a saddle and grace a hunting-field. "I shall have Mary and Jenny taught immediately now," said a lady to me one day in the course of last summer,--"They shall have a pony a-piece, and John (the groom) shall teach them." Of course, I said nothing, my principle of noninterference standing me in good stead; but when an hour or so later, I beheld the said John disporting himself, and showing off his equestrian skill upon one of the carriage-horses, I really felt pity for the two charming little girls who were so soon to be handed over to his doubtful tuition.

And now for the third portion of your correspondent's letter: namely, the question of the straight saddle. "H. de V. R." says he has never seen any such; and I consider this extremely probable, for he will recollect my saying that a saddle such as I described should be made to order, as it is certainly not in general use--but I am not altogether singular in my advocacy of it. Peat and Co., Piccadilly, or Box and Co., Abbey Street, Dublin, will manufacture saddles of this description in excellent style, but only to order, for they have not yet found sufficient favour--or, to express it better, are not sufficiently known--to have become popular, and manufacturers therefore will not keep them in stock. The advantages of a straight saddle are manifold. Firstly, it is the only means by which a lady can learn the necessary art of riding from balance. This can be acquired by sitting *on* a saddle, but never by sitting *in* one. Secondly, she can, when riding upon a straight saddle, change and shift her position, which as a necessary consequence changes her weight upon the horse's back, and saves him from being galled. A noble lady wrote to me some time since, "I know not how it is; all my horses are laid up with sore backs; and yet my saddle is well padded." I guessed the secret at once; she was riding in a sort of well, or chair, from which her heavy weight could never for an instant shift, and hence the trouble of which she complained. I sent her a sketch of my saddle, with the address of the man who had made it, and she has since been a staunch upholder of my theory. Thirdly, the best figure in the world would look to disadvantage if seated in a saddle with a dip or slope; whereas a well-made woman, attired in a habit properly fitted about the waist and hips, never looks to such complete advantage as when sitting gracefully and at ease upon a well constructed straight-made saddle. Fourthly, if in taking an up-jump the horse misses his footing and struggles in an unsuccessful effort to recover himself, the lady may--if riding upon a straight saddle--succeed in slipping from it to a situation of comparative safety; but, if she has a high projection of iron and stiff leather just behind her, it bars her movement, and as a consequence the horse falls back *upon* her, and catching her between his weight and the edge of the ditch or furrow, as the case may be, injures her spine, sometimes fatally, and frequently in a serious manner.

The question, "Do I also advocate straight saddles for men's use?" is answered by my reminding "H. de V. R." that there is no analogy between a gentleman's position upon horseback and that of a lady. What would be a necessity, or at least a *luxury*, for the one would be eminently unsuited for the other. A man's superior activity and greater liberty of motion place him ever at an advantage. And whilst upon this subject I would strongly urge upon all humane riders, especially the male portion of them, to have their saddles made high *in front*, so as not to press upon the horse's withers, causing him much needless suffering. A space capable of accommodating at least two fingers should be between withers and saddle, and were this attended to we should see fewer skin abrasions and unsightly lumps upon poor submissive animals, and less of that stuffing of handkerchiefs between cruel leather and bleeding flesh which so frequently pains the sorrowing eyes of sensitive and pitying persons.

I think I have now dealt fully with "H. de V. R.'s" letter, and must thank the writer of it for his complimentary observations, and his kindly appreciation of my labours in a cause which I certainly have very much at heart.

Apologising for trespassing thus far upon your valuable space.

I am, Sir,

Yours obediently,

NANNIE POWER O'DONAGHUE.

October 12, 1880.

* * * * *

SIR,--Many readers of *The Illustrated Sporting and Dramatic News* hope that Mrs. Power O'Donoghue, in her very interesting letters upon "Ladies on Horseback," will touch fully on the most important thing, viz. "the ladies' horse." One sees ladies riding all sorts; some too big, some too small, some good shoulders and no backs, others just the reverse; not one out of twenty what it ought to be. Also, up to what weight should it be? What is the average weight of ladies, and the difference in ordinary dress to the habit? It is often said that, owing to the peculiar seat, the weight being all on one side, a lady tires a horse much more than a man; certainly you often see ladies' horses going short with the near hind leg, possibly from this cause. Could not the weight of side-saddles be reduced? Those used by the Empress of Austria could not have weighed 8 lb., and she was herself a light woman. Anything on this subject will interest many readers.

I am, &c.

EQUES.

* * * * *

SIR,--There is one point to which I should like to call the attention of the writer of the able and interesting articles on "Ladies on Horseback," which she appears to have altogether overlooked in her enumeration of the articles of a lady's riding attire. It is the use of a spur by lady equestrians. The recently invented lady's spur consists of one sharp point so constructed as not to injure the habit. In hunting, a spur is indispensable, and in park-riding is very desirable for a lady, who has so much less control over her horse than a man. Young girls just beginning to ride will find the use of a spur most beneficial in managing their steeds. Hired horses are never altogether to be trusted, and in the case of their showing temper or laziness, two or three pricks with a lady's spur will subdue them far more quickly than the application of a whip. I have more than once ridden a horse that was a confirmed jibber, and have always found a few determined thrusts with my spur, combined with an efficiently applied whip, never failed to bring him down. I confidently recommend all ladies, and especially young girls just beginning the art of equitation, to procure a lady's spur, and never to mount a horse without it.

I am, &c.

MABEL FLORENCE RAYNE.

The Firs, Cheltenham,

Oct. 18th, 1880.

* * * * *

SIR,--I suppose it would be impossible to advance any opinions to which there would not be objections raised, but I write, not in a cavilling spirit, but as one really anxious for information, to know whether Mrs. Power O'Donoghue would seriously advocate striking a horse between the ears when it rears. Surely such a thing would be exceedingly dangerous for any lady to attempt, and, as your correspondent is writing solely for ladies, I conclude she refers to them in the present instance. I feel very strongly upon this point, because an uncle of mine, some years ago, when out riding tried this experiment at the advice of a friend. The horse (not a vicious one) suddenly reared; my uncle loosened the reins and urged it forward, but finding this ineffectual, struck it violently between the ears with his hunting-whip. The animal, maddened, I presume, by the pain, reared straight on end and fell backward; its rider being a very agile man, slipped off sideways, and thus escaped nearly certain death; but had the rider been a lady instead of a gentleman the consequences must have been fatal; and with so light a switch as a lady usually carries, a blow between the ears could only serve to irritate without producing any good effect. I would ask one more question: Why does your correspondent so strongly object to the use of the "old-fashioned slipper" stirrup? I am rather curious on this point, because I have ever since the tender age of four, when my riding experiences began, used the shoe-stirrup, and I have always thought it so safe, because my foot slips out in a second. I am aware that it is extremely unfashionable, as in Rotton Row you hardly see a lady using it; but I keep to it still, not so much with the idea of its safety, but for comfort, especially in trotting. I find it extremely difficult to keep an iron stirrup from slipping back into the instep, and, being used to rise pressing on the toes, I think that rising from the instep is more difficult and doubles the exertion of trotting. In conclusion, I must express a hope that Mrs. Power O'Donoghue will not give me credit for writing in a spirit of unfriendly criticism; but as I am exceedingly fond of riding, I feel an interest in working out this subject to its fullest extent. I am sure all lady riders must feel grateful to Mrs. Power O'Donoghue for the valuable and useful instructions contained in her interesting letters, and one has only to pay a visit to the Row between 12 and 2 in the season, to see how much they are needed by the generality of the "ladies on horseback."

I am, &c.

EQUESTRINA.

October 13th, 1880.

* * * * *

SIR,--Though not an "aggrieved stirrup-maker," it may not be out of place if I, as a saddler of many years' experience and a great lover of horses, offer a few comments on the "hints and instructions" set forth in your paper for the benefit of ladies on horseback, written by one of the sex who is evidently an authority on the subject she treats so ably. There is no doubt these articles will be read with great interest by very many ladies who desire to acquit themselves well on horseback, and also by their gentlemen friends who are anxious to conduce to the safety and comfort of their fair companions in that delightful exercise, but cannot have the same knowledge to impart the theoretical instructions now given by your lady writer, whose criticisms will therefore be valuable to both. In following her remarks, it occurs to me that I may perhaps venture on a little comment without being considered too intrusive. The objection taken to children riding is no doubt formed on good grounds, but I think that with care young ladies might be permitted at a much earlier age than sixteen to acquire some practice in the saddle; it is true that young girls are liable to curvature of the spine, when allowed to ride day after day on the same side of their pony, but I have understood that this danger is obviated by changing their position to the other side on alternate days, and I should be glad to learn what are the objections to this. It seems to me rather desirable that ladies should have equal facility in riding on either side, but there may be reasons against it of which I am ignorant. This lady says that the nicest bridle for a beginner is a plain ring-snaffle, but states further that few horses will go in it; the latter remark, if correct, (which I should venture to doubt), raises a fatal objection to the ring-snaffle, as I fear that not one young lady in twenty, under amateur teaching, would be put upon a perfectly trained nag, desirable as this must be; and thus an ordinary stout mouth plain snaffle, or plain bar with single rein, would surely be preferable. I fancy it would be found of much advantage if riding was taught in the first instance without the use of reins at all, the horse simply being led by an attendant; the learner thus gets a proper balance, without depending on the bridle for support, as many are found to do. For a young girl I should like to know what is the objection to a pad, or pilch as they are called, made for use on either side. These, having no tree, are nearly level, but there is perhaps a chance of its turning round if the rider does not sit straight; for a grown girl, the properly made saddle is better every way. In common with your correspondent "H. de V. R.," I fail quite to understand how a side-saddle is to be made "as straight as a board." A saddle is made on a foundation, or tree, of wood and iron, which should be shaped for the back intended to bear it, and must be raised slightly in front for the wither and behind to clear the backbone; but it is right that the seat should be as level as possible. This is probably the lady's meaning. It is very essential that the saddle should fit the horse correctly and be of suitable size and shape for the rider; the former consideration is too often overlooked and thus entails discomfort to both. There are saddles, and saddles, as ladies often find to their cost. A very large proportion in use here, and more abroad, are put together in Birmingham and Walsall on the slop system; they will please the eyes of an inexperienced purchaser, but are formed with little regard to the requirements of the poor animals who suffer under them, or of their riders' comfort, and it is probable that these are the saddles against which ladies are very properly warned. It is really indispensable for a lady's comfort in riding that she should have a good saddle, made by a competent and conscientious saddler, whose business it is to see that it is suitable. Considering the number of years that a good saddle with care will last, it is inconceivable that the comparatively small additional price should be grudged for a perfect and satisfactory article by a maker of repute, instead of the machine-made slop rubbish, by which many a good animal is injured and the temper of his rider seriously chafed. Enough about saddles for the present, so I will go to the next point under discussion--the stirrup. Your lady rider must have been very unfortunate in her use of the safety-stirrup, which, in my opinion, does in practice usually justify its name. I have known very many instances in which ladies have owed immunity from serious accident to its use. As "H. de V. R." justly says, the mechanism of the stirrup (which is very simple) should not be allowed to get out of order by neglect; surely the lady or her friends, particularly if so "knowledgeable" as the writer of the article, might [They "*might*." That they so often do not, and that danger so frequently results from the neglect, is the grievance and complaint of our contributor.--ED. *I.S. & D.N.*] take the trouble personally to see that her stirrup is not out of order from rust, and in no other way but one can it be so; the other way is that if the groom ignorantly or carelessly adjusts the stirrup for use hind part before, the inner stirrup cannot be released, and the rider's foot, in case of a fall, will be helplessly fixed in the stirrup. This eventuality, however, does not detract from the real value of the safety-stirrup, for neglect and ignorance will entail direful consequences in all ways. Next to the safety-stirrup, I quite believe that a plain steel stirrup of suitable size, with side pieces at the bottom to take sharp pressure off the foot, is the most suitable for ladies' use, and I always condemn the small padded stirrup, which is, indeed, a fruitful source of danger to lady riders.

With the rest of Mrs. O'Donoghue's dissertation I cordially agree, and believe it would be beneficial if both men and ladies practised riding without the aid of the stirrup; and the same rule applies to and is generally practised by men, as I saw a few days ago on a German barrack-ground, where an awkward squad was being trained in that manner. The art of putting a lady up is one that should be practised more than it is by horsemen; my first attempt resulted in the lady slipping down again, and on my hat, which suffered even more than my self-esteem. On one occasion in the Crimea, years ago, I was riding with a lady and her husband, the former dismounted at Mrs. Seacole's for refreshment, and on being put up again by her husband with more vigour than skill, the poor lady was sent over her horse's back to the ground on the other side, and being somewhat portly, was shaken severely. I fear many ladies have suffered in the same way from the awkwardness of their attendants, but I have seen ladies so agile as to mount from the ground without assistance--rather a difficult feat, and requiring much practice. Having trespassed so much on your space I must not proceed further now, but shall be happy to air my notions again, if agreeable to your readers and riders.

Yours, &c.

JERMYN.

* * * * *

SIR,--My papers entitled "Ladies on Horseback" have called forth many letters. Some of these you have printed, some have been forwarded to me from your office, and many have been received at my own house. I shall regard it as a favour if you will permit me to reply to a few of them through the medium of your paper, as in answering one I shall answer many who have written upon the same subject.

J. V.--When the horse took head with me and leaped into the farm-yard (as depicted by Mr. Sturgess) I had no way of getting out except by the passage and kitchen of the farm-house, as the gates of the yard were locked, and the owner of the place--who was away at the neighbouring town--had the key in his pocket.

EQUES.--The reason why ladies ride "all sorts of horses" is that comparatively few keep horses of their own, and those who are without them and are fond of riding, jump eagerly at the offer of a friend's mount, whether it be suitable or otherwise. A nice horse for a lady may be thus described: Height about 15-3; Colour dark bay or brown, well-set sloping shoulders, good back, arched loins, firm and graceful neck, small head and ears, shapely clean-cut legs, and good firm feet. A horse of this description will be well up to 13 or 14 st. For a heavy weight an animal should be selected with a short wide back, powerful quarters, big healthy hocks, and stoutly-built fore-legs. The *average* weight of ladies is about 9st. Summer costume and riding gear would weigh about equally, but velvet or sealskin would outweigh a habit. A lady seated upon a properly-made saddle, if she has been well taught, will never have her weight "all on one side." The reason why horses go short with the near hind leg is because ladies ride from the stirrup, leaning their full weight upon it, and galling the animal's back. The stirrup is meant to assist, not to *support*, the rider. Old-fashioned side-saddles are all too heavy; but a well-constructed modern saddle can scarcely be improved upon. It is a mistake to ride in too light a saddle, as it brings the weight of the body too near the horse's back. That used by the Empress of Austria weighed 12 lbs., which is about a correct standard.

LADYBIRD.--Nobody who has any regard for life and limb now rides through Dublin. All wise persons gave it up when pavement and tram-lines made the city what it is. Consequently the park is deserted, and only a solitary horseman is seen in Stephen's Green.

INQUIRER.--The shoe should be made to *fit the foot*. It is most cruel, and is a fruitful source of lameness, to pare the foot away to make it fit a ready-made shoe. If you cannot trust your farrier, change him. This advice also applies to JAMES R., but I do not undertake to answer questions respecting the treatment or management of the horse.

MABEL FLORENCE RAYNE.--I had not forgotten nor overlooked the important uses of the spur. You will find the subject treated in my papers upon hunting and hunting-costume. I do not, however, *at all* approve of its use for beginners, as such are certain, through nervousness, to press the left heel close to the horse's side, and, if furnished with a spur, would cause him much needless pain and irritation, besides endangering their own safety.

ROBERT KEATING.--Best thanks for letter and papers.

G. ELLIOT.--For riding with a bit and bridoon, place a rein between each finger of your left hand, and hold them securely with your thumb, reserving your right hand for your whip; or take your reins in both hands, and ride your horse upon the curb, or snaffle, according to his temperament. For riding with a single rein, place the near leather under your little finger and the off one between the first and second fingers, which is as good a way as any; but I have already said that there is no fixed rule for holding reins, and a good rider will constantly change them about, and move the bridle in her horse's mouth, which prevents him hanging upon his bit.

JANE CARR.--I scarcely know whether to regard your letter as a compliment or the reverse. My labours have been *totally* unassisted; nor has my experience of this world shown me that its occupants are sufficiently philanthropic to labour that another may reap the merit and the reward.

L. K.--The subject is not within my province. Mayhew's *Horse Management*, published by Allen & Co., 13, Waterloo Place, London, is the best I can recommend.

HUNTSMAN.--It is for ladies I am writing.

ELEANOR.--Thanks; but if I adopted one half of the suggestions offered, a strange result would ensue. Happily my papers went to press without *anybody* (save the Editor) having had a glance at them. He generously accepted them upon their merits; but had I shown them to others I should either have altered something in every second line or have given offence to numerous well-meaning persons. When I was a child I committed to memory the inimitable fable of "The Miller, his Son, and his Ass," and have taken the moral of it as a guide through life.

GOODALL.--A short hunting-crop without a lash would do.

EQUESTRINA.--If a horse rears with me in a vicious manner I hit him between the ears, but I do not by any means expect my readers to coincide in all my views, and those who know a better plan can, of course, adopt it. If an animal rears slightly I lean forward against his neck, touch him with my heel, and speak to him. If he persists, and I see any danger of his falling back, I hit him between the ears with the butt-end of my whip, not sufficiently heavily to "madden him," nor even to cause him the least pain, but to occasion him to duck his head, which he invariably does; and if at that instant I hit him sharply with my heel, he drops at once and lashes out behind. Allowing for a moment that such a mode of action may be open to objection, is it not better (seeing that it is frequently efficacious) than sitting quietly and permitting one's-self to be fallen back upon, without making any effort to avert the catastrophe? My objection to the slipper-stirrup is founded on the knowledge that it encourages ladies to lean their weight upon it. "It feels so comfortable," I heard a lady say, "so like a resting-board beneath my foot, that I *cannot help* riding from it." An iron stirrup with the foot well home is the proper thing to ride in; and remember it is from the instep and *not* from the toes that you should rise. The iron should meet the waist of the boot-sole, and a long flat heel (I do not mean one of those atrocities known as a *high* one) should be worn on the boot.

JERMYN.--Your letter almost answers itself. The pad or pilch *is* apt to turn round, for it is only one little girl in twenty who sits straight. You judge my meaning rightly about the straight saddle, but I opine that it is the stuffing which should be arranged to guard the backbone from pressure, and that it is in no way necessary to raise the *seat* at the back. I must again say, for the third time, that a plain ring-snaffle is the *nicest* for a lady's use, and also maintain my opinion that few horses will go in it, according to *my* ideas of "going." A horse who goes well in a ring-snaffle must have a perfect temper and a perfect mouth, a combination as rare in the equine as in the human tribe. For ordinary hunters and roadsters I do not recommend it, simply because they will not go in such a bridle; but I shall ever hold to my opinion that it is the nicest and the least puzzling for a beginner.

KATIE.--Not worth denying. It is one of those worthless untruths which I have long since learned to treat with contempt.

LIVERPUDLIAN.--Your suggestion is so good that I shall certainly adopt it. Nothing could be better adapted for riding in than a warm jersey, buttoned in front. Being elastic it would allow full play for the arms and shoulders, and would also display a good figure to advantage. If you, or some other, would only get up a sufficient amount of courage to turn a deaf ear to the hateful and oft-recurring "What will be said?" we might have many useful and elegant innovations of which at present we know nothing.

YOUNG WIFE.--There can be no impropriety in what you say. "Honi soit qui mal y pense?" So long as you have a good conscience and your husband's approval you need care little for what the world says.

X. Y. Z., DASHAWAY, and COUNTRYMAN.--I cannot reply to your letters.

Thanking you, Sir, for your kindness in granting me so much of your valuable space,

I am, &c.

NANNIE POWER O'DONOGHUE.

October 25.

* * * * *

SIR,--The "recently-invented lady's spur," mentioned in your last issue by "Mabel Florence Kayne," was patented towards the close of the last century, and illustrations of it, and of other spurs on the same principle, can be seen at the Patent Office. I quite concur in the recommendation that a lady should always wear a spur, and it will be seen from the last article by Mrs. Power O'Donoghue that a spur forms part of her hunting equipment; but I strongly advise ladies to wear a spur with a rowel having only five points, which should be long and sharp. The spur with one point and a spring sheath is commonly sold by saddlers for ladies' use, but is liable to break or get out of order, and is always discarded in favour of the one with a five-pointed rowel by ladies who have tried the latter. Mrs. Power O'Donoghue is doing good service to ladies by protesting against the stirrups facetiously so-called "safety." I always advise a lady to use a perfectly plain steel stirrup, but a tolerably heavy one. Why cannot the stirrup be attached to a lady's saddle in the same manner as to a gentleman's? Then, in case of accident, the stirrup and leather would come away together. An excellent bit for a lady's horse is a curb-bit, suspended in the horse's mouth by two large rings, to which the snaffle-reins are also attached. This bit is very light or very severe, at the rider's wish.

I am, &c.

SOUTHERN CROSS.

October 26, 1880.

* * * * *

SIR,--Continuing my remarks on this subject, I am bound to say that your contributor gives sufficient answer to the question of the safety-stirrup in explaining that the objection is removed providing the inner stirrup is large enough for the foot to be easily extricated; the stirrup being made in three different sizes, this is a matter easily adjusted. The shoe-stirrup referred to by "Equestrina" was in use by ladies for many years, and in point of safety I think no objection can be raised to it; the same shape of stirrup is much affected by men in South America.

The instructions in Part Second of Mrs. Power O'Donoghue's writings are very admirable, except that I do not see the utility of a lady's striking a rearing horse between the ears, with the few ounces of whip usually carried. I have known men do so with a loaded whip, and knocking a horse down to cure him of this vice, but it would be scarcely advisable for a lady to try this. I am rather surprised to see it stated as a fact that both rearing and plunging maybe entirely prevented by using the so-called anti-rearing bit martingale. It certainly may prevent rearing on the first attempt if the horse's head is kept down tightly by this martingale attached to the breastplate, but as the latter is seldom worn except for hunting, it cannot be intended to recommend it for that purpose, for it would infallibly follow that the fixed martingale would bring both horse and rider to grief at the very first fence they attempted to clear, and if the horse had sufficient liberty of action to jump freely, the martingale would be no obstruction to his rearing. I know from my own experience that a horse can be knocked down by a blow on the head. I was once doing a little private mounted practice at sword exercise, preparatory to a prize competition, and grasping my sword with thick gloves on, the weapon somehow turned in my hand, caught my mare below the ear on the bridle-hand, and knocked her completely off her legs, to our mutual amazement, though no great harm was done. I do not see what analogy there can be between the powerful Chifney bit and a rearing martingale; the effect of the latter may be secured by attaching a split martingale, with leather or spring billets, to the mouth-rings of any bit in use, snaffle or Pelham; but I believe that a horse can, if determined, rear all the same, and it certainly would not prevent plunging or bucking. For a restive or jibbing horse in saddle I have always found a short running martingale very useful; the rider should shorten and lower the right rein well down the horse's shoulder, apply the right leg and spur sharply, and turn the horse round like a teetotum until he is dizzy, then give him both spurs when his head is in the right direction. This will set him going before he knows where he is, and is a practice I have found very efficacious, but not easily applicable by ladies.

On the subject of bits, my own favourite is the Hanoverian Pelham; it will generally hold the strongest puller, and, with a light hand, I have never met a horse that would not face it. For show or park riding there is none better; it is, however, not suited to those who trust to the bridle-reins for their balance in the saddle.

"Eques" inquires "what is the average weight of ladies?" This is a difficult query, but as ladies ride at all weights between six and eleven stone, with a margin each way, I should suppose the average would be about 8-1/2 stone, exclusive of saddle, &c. A lady who is an indifferent rider would throw more weight on one side than the other, one cause of so many sore backs from side-saddles; but a thoroughly good horsewoman would sit with as level a balance as a man. The weight of good modern side-saddles is much reduced, but they cannot well be made under 14 lb., with furniture, and are usually considerably more. If the Empress of Austria uses a saddle of 8 lb. only (as some have averred), she must ride on a man's steeplechase-saddle, which perhaps would not be a difficult performance for a lady who is said to be in the habit of driving four-in-hand.

I am much impressed by the recital of your contributor's adventures and hair-breadth escapes on the saddle, particularly on the occasion she refers to when invited by a friend to ride the big bay horse. If the friend was a gentleman, I must repeat the opinion I heard expressed by a lady when reading the article--that any man who would wilfully expose a woman to risk her life on such a brute behaved disgracefully. There is no object in creation to my mind more attractive than a graceful woman controlling with ease a fine and well-trained horse; but no one with due respect for the sex would wish to see her taking the place of a rough rider.

Yours, &c.

JERMYN.

* * * * *

SIR,--Although I care nothing for anything that may be said about myself, I am ever loyal to my friends, and it seems to me hard that one of the truest of them should be spoken of as having "behaved disgracefully" by a writer who, with more impetuosity than judgment, jumps at conclusions without waiting to hear the truth. When I was riding homeward after the leap into the farm-yard, I met the owner of the horse upon the road, driving out with a friend. The moment he heard what had occurred he took me off the animal, changed my saddle to the very quiet horse he was driving, and actually, after nearly an hour's delay, succeeded in putting the harness upon the "big bay," and, having done so, drove him home regardless of his own safety, or rather of his danger, which was imminent. I do not think there are many men at his time of life, and in his delicate state of health, who would have done the same thing rather than chance a second runaway. He had *no* reason to suppose that any such thing would, in the first instance, have happened, and I believe it was attributable to the fact that the horse had been ridden a day or two previously by a very wild rider, who had spoilt his mouth and manners, and who subsequently apologised to me for having been the cause of what occurred. I might have mentioned all this before, and certainly should have done so had I thought that such necessity should have arisen. I would remind "Jermyn" that my observations respecting the martingale were confined to my papers on *road-riding*, not on hunting, and would also thank him, with my best obeisance, for calling me a rough-rider.

I am, Sir,

Yours obediently,

NANNIE POWER O'DONOGHUE.

October 31, 1880.

* * * * *

SIR,--I must, in justice to myself, ask you to be so kind as to grant me space in your influential journal to reply to the very serious charge "Jermyn" brought against me in your issue of the 30th of the past month. I am the friend who asked Mrs. Power O'Donoghue to ride "the big bay," and yet I believe that nobody in all the world has a higher esteem for that lady, nor a truer regard for her safety than I have. Indeed there are few men in Ireland (if one) worth being called the name, who would not willingly lay down their own lives rather than imperil the life of one so universally beloved. The horse up to the day of the runaway had been perfectly quiet and most easily managed. He carried me two seasons to hounds, never making a mistake nor pulling in the least. Not being able to ride, having shortly before met with a very serious accident, I lent "the big bay" to a hard-riding young officer for a day's hunting. He unfortunately must have made too free use of his long-necked spurs, and, totally unknown to me, ruffled the horse's temper; the animal remembering the treatment he received, and finding but a feather on his back, when excited by the music of the hounds, overpowered his rider; but, thank Heaven, no serious accident occurred. I was unutterably shocked and distressed on hearing of the occurrence, and may state that on the day in question I was driving in my dog-cart, accompanied by a gentleman (late an officer in Her Majesty's service) who can vouch for the truth of my statement, when Mrs. O'Donoghue came up to me and told me of her very narrow escape. I did not hesitate an instant to say, "I will take out the horse I am driving. You know him to be a perfect mount, and I will put 'the big bay' in my trap." The lady did not wish me to do so, knowing the risk I ran in putting a horse in harness that had never been in such before. I at last succeeded in prevailing on her not to lose the day's sport, changed the saddle with great difficulty, and attached "the big bay" to my dog-cart; after a few plunges and an endeavour to get away, he settled down, and has since gone grandly. My friend, though a very bold man, would not get in with me for some time. I hope after this explanation your correspondent will be sufficiently generous to allow that I did all in my power to insure the safety of a most precious life. With regard to the term "rough-rider," as applied by "Jermyn" to Mrs. O'Donoghue, I feel assured if he knew the lady he would not for worlds have used such an expression.

I am, Sir,

Your most obedient servant,

ONE WHO HAS RIDDEN TO HOUNDS FOR OVER SIXTY YEARS.

* * * * *

SIR,--I should by no means recommend a young lady to wear a spur when learning in a riding-school, but from my own experience I strongly advise all girls beginning to ride on the road never to mount their steeds without a sharp spur on their left boot. The second time I went out riding, when I was fourteen, my cob, startled by some noise, suddenly began to rear and pitch vigorously. I applied my whip sharply across his flank, but without effect. I then gave him a series of sharp pricks with my spur, which completely subdued him. Had I been without a spur I should probably have been thrown and severely injured. I should certainly prefer a spur with a rowel as "Southern Cross" recommends, but would it not be apt to tear the habit?

I am, &c.

MABEL FLORENCE RAYNE.

The Firs, Cheltenham,

November 1, 1880.

* * * * *

SIR,--A correspondent in your last number advises ladies to use a rowel spur, with five prongs, long and sharp, so, as a friend of horses, I am inclined to write an objection to their taking this advice. In the first place, from the nature of a lady's seat, her armed heel would often unintentionally irritate and annoy the horse; and in the second place many would probably use this instrument of torture too severely, and therefore cruelly. A rowel spur, with five long and sharp prongs--in fact, a jockey's spur--is a much more severe instrument than is required for ordinary riding, either by man or woman, and the advantage of the ladies' bore spur is, that it can only be applied when intended, and then is quite sufficiently severe. I have no objection to ladies, who are good horsewomen, wearing a spur, and using it, too, as severely as necessary, but I have great objections to any unnecessary pain or annoyance being given to my friends, the horses. Another lady correspondent of yours says that a spur is quite indispensable for hunting. If she means that it should always be worn in case it is required, I agree; but I have ridden a courageous high-tempered horse for years with hounds without ever using the spur.

I am, &c.

FAIR PLAY.

Glasgow, 1st November 1880.

* * * * *

SIR,--As the subject of spurs and other riding equipment for ladies seems at the present time to occupy and interest many of your fair readers, permit me, on behalf of my sisters, who are horsewomen of some experience, both at home and in the colonies, and who have practically tried most known riding-costumes, to recommend, through the medium of your columns, the following as a comfortable and serviceable riding-dress for a lady, for long country rides, picnics, &c.; of course not for the Park, or a lawn meet. Habit--a short, strong hunting-skirt, short enough to walk in with comfort, with jacket of same cloth as skirt, made loose enough to admit of a jersey being worn under it if required; a wide leather belt for the waist, fastening with a buckle. This belt will be found a great comfort and support when on horseback for many hours. Hat of soft felt, or a melon-shaped hat. Pantaloons of chamois leather, buttoning close at the ankles. Hussar or Wellington boots, reaching to about four inches of the knee, to be worn over the pantaloons, made of Peel leather with *moderate*-sized heels, tipped with brass, and soles strong but not thick. A leather stud should be sewn on the left boot, about 2-1/2 inches above the heel, on which stud the spur should rest, and thus be kept in its place without tight buckling. The spur found to be the most useful after the trial of many is a rowel spur of plated steel, about two inches to two and-a-half inches long, strong and light, hunting shape, and fastened with a strap and buckle, the foot-strap of plated steel chain. This chain foot-strap looks neater than a leather one, and does not become cut or worn out when on foot on rough or rocky ground. The rowel pin is a screw pin; thus the rowel can be changed at pleasure, and a sharp or a blunt one fitted as is required by the horse one rides. The spur I mention can be obtained of Messrs. Maxwell & Co., Piccadilly, London; or of Mr. Thompson, saddler, Dawson street, Dublin.

Some ladies affect two spurs--one, the right, being fitted with a blank rowel; this is, of course, for appearance sake when dismounted. I have not often seen two spurs worn. I am not alluding to Miss Bird's riding-costume, as described in her books, *Life in the Sandwich Islands* and *The Rocky Mountains*. She rode *à la cavalière*, in a Mexican saddle, and wearing big rowel Mexican spurs, and appears from her account to have preferred this style of riding to the modern style and side-saddle. Some years ago I saw a photograph of the Queen of Naples (I think in 1860), representing the queen mounted *à la cavalière*, wearing a high felt hat, a long white cloak, patent-leather jack-boots, and gilt spurs. Can any of your readers inform me if this style of riding for ladies is a custom of Southern Italy as well as Mexico and the Sandwich Islands?

I am, &c.

JACK SPUR.

* * * * *

SIR,--I cannot regret that my letter has given the authoress of this work, and also the owner of the "big bay" horse, an opportunity of explaining the circumstances attending her mount on that puissant but headstrong animal, and of repudiating the erroneous construction put upon it, as probably the same idea may have occurred to many other readers of the anecdote, who may not have cared to express their sentiments. I must say, however, that I am very sorry if my remarks occasioned pain to either of your correspondents. The explanation given shows clearly that no blame was really attributable to the gentleman who offered the mount, and I can well believe he never dreamt of danger with the horse in such skilful hands. No one would doubt the sincerity of the statement given, that the horse was put in harness for the first time and driven away, after such an experience of his temper; but it speaks more highly for the courage than discretion of his owner, and I can well understand the friend's hesitation to share the driving-seat, for there are few things more trying to the nerves than to sit behind a determined bolter. Perhaps I write feelingly, having been in that predicament myself three years ago, resulting in a fractured hip and permanent lameness. I will most certainly admit that the chivalrous gentleman did all, and more than was necessary, to avert further peril to the lady who had so narrow an escape. As for the obnoxious term "rough rider," to which exception is taken, it was intended to be used generally and not individually; if it has unfortunately happened that Mrs. Power O'Donoghue, whom I have never had the pleasure of seeing, took it in a personal sense, I most sincerely beg her forgiveness, and will ask her rather to accept, as applicable to herself, the earlier remarks about ladies on horseback at the conclusion of my letter, and the assurance of my belief that such a gentlewoman as she is described could never be a *rough* rider in any way.

I am, &c.

JERMYN.

* * * * *

SIR,--The spur with a five-pointed rowel was strongly recommended for ladies' use many years ago in the *Queen*, and is worn by many: it does not tear the habit, and is not more severe than the spring-sheath spur with a point of the same length, as only one point of the rowel can prick the horse at a time; indeed, it is not so severe, as it can be applied with a very slight touch, which generally is all that is required, whilst the spring-sheath spur must be applied with sufficient force to overcome the resistance of the spring, with the result that the horse is often more sharply pricked than the rider intends. The points of a lady's spur should be long enough to be effective if the skirt of the habit intervenes, as, with any arrangement, it sometimes will do, when, if the points are too short, the horse does not feel it. I dissent from the statement of "Fairplay" that, "from the nature of a lady's seat, her armed heel would often unintentionally irritate and annoy her horse." If applied to a clumsy rider the statement is accurate, but a lady who is a moderately good rider has no difficulty in keeping her foot in the proper position, and a lady's left foot should be in the same position as a man's; whilst, as a lady has the third crutch to steady her left leg, she has less excuse than a man would have for the unintentional use of the spur; but this evil carries its own antidote, for the lady would soon perceive the result of the irritation, and become more careful. The best way to cure a boy of turning out his toes and holding on with his heels is to give him a pair of long-necked spurs, and then put him on a fidgetty horse; a few minutes' experience teaches him more than a month of lecturing. I never knew of a mishap occurring to a lady through accidentally spurring her horse, but I have known many instances of ladies being put to great inconvenience and annoyance through not wearing a spur, and I do not understand why a lady should be more likely than a man to use it with undue severity. That it is an advantage to a lady is clearly shown by the fact that a lady who once tries one always continues its use. "Fairplay" is also mistaken about the spring-sheath spur, for it is as readily applied as any other, though more force is required, which is objectionable, and especially so in park riding, when the spring of the horse to an unintentionally sharp application betrays the action of the rider. I claim to be as good a friend of horses as "Fairplay," but I have some regard for the rider as well as for the horse, and I consider that, whilst we are justified in riding horses, we are justified in using such reasonable aids as we find most satisfactory to ourselves; and I have no sympathy with anyone who objects to a lady availing herself of the convenience and assistance so readily supplied by a judiciously-used spur, which every horseman knows cannot, in very many cases, be obtained by any other means, and which he never hesitates to avail himself of. In these days of locomotion a lady loses a great deal of the pleasures of travelling, and of the opportunities of seeing the countries she may visit, unless she can and will ride such horses as she may meet with in those countries; and even in the rural districts of England there is many an old nag of the "Proputty Proputty" type, which (though not possessed of the special points of a lady's horse--"Oh! such a lovely mane and tail") will carry a lady tolerably well if he feels the spur occasionally. If "Mabel Florence Rayne" tries the rowel spur and the bit I mentioned in my former letter, I am sure she will be satisfied with them, and perhaps she will write her opinion for the benefit of others. The excellent and sensible letters of Mrs. Power O'Donoghue will probably convince people that a horse, when he has a lady on his back, is very much the same kind of animal, and requires very much the same kind of management, as when he is ridden by a man. If Mrs. Power O'Donoghue can obtain this result, she will sweep away many of the peculiar prejudices and ideas that now prevail as to all matters appertaining to ladies on horseback.

I am, &c.

SOUTHERN CROSS.

* * * * *

SIR,--In the article under the above-mentioned heading, published in your issue of the 6th November, Mrs. Power O'Donoghue recommends that horses' tails should not be docked. Dealers, when offering horses for sale, do not usually volunteer any information as to whether the horses have been docked. I wish, therefore, to inform any intending purchasers who may not know how to ascertain whether a horse has been docked, and who may wish to obtain some which have not been disfigured in this manner, that if the dock (that is, the portion of the tail which consists of bones and muscles, &c.) is in its natural state, the hair grows thickly at the end or tip of it, and there is no bare space there; but if it has been shortened by a portion of it being cut off (or docked), there is at the end or tip of it a circular space of about an inch in diameter, entirely bare of hair. When a horse has been docked, the hair of the tail scarcely grows after it has reached to within six or seven inches above the hocks. The hocks of a large horse are about twenty-five inches above the ground. It is a general custom with London dealers to cut the hair of the tail very short before offering a horse for sale, so that it does not come down lower than to a distance of about nine inches above the hocks. The buyer cannot then tell to what length the tail is likely to grow. If customers would refuse to buy horses with the hair of the tail cut short, perhaps the practice in question would be discontinued by the dealers.

I am, Sir, &c.

X. Y. Z.

London, November 10, 1880.

* * * * *

SIR,--In your paper of last week I notice a letter on the advisability of ladies on horseback adopting the cross-saddle in place of the side, that is to say, in plain English, ride astride. This I have done abroad when far beyond conventional bondage, and it is incomparably better. Your correspondent points out the evils resulting from the one-sided twisted seat, which a lady now has, and also, in the same paper, the authoress of *Ladies on Horseback* says how impossible it is with only one foot in the stirrup to rise comfortably to a high trotter. Now I should never have dared to name such a change had it not been thus mooted. Society will shriek out and say, "Woman would be indeed out of place thus." Why? I am sure with a proper dress there is nothing to hurt the extremely proper feelings of the most modest. All who have hunted know that the *very* short skirted habits at times display, well, say the leg of the fair *equestrienne* most liberally. Now the dress for the cross-horse style is much the same as a bathing suit, loose Zouave drawers drawn close below the knee, and fastened tightly over the boot at the ankle; a loose tunic, long enough to come almost to the knee when mounted, lightly belted at the waist, a cape falling over the shoulders, not quite to the elbows. This is my attire when free to ride in the *only* really comfortable way, a foot in each stirrup. Oh, no woman would ever be twisted and packed on to a side saddle again if she could help it, after once enjoying the ease and freedom, as well as complete control of her horse which a man's seat gives.

So far as exhibitions of limbs go, it is much more delicate, and there is nothing to offend the most sensitive lady in this style. Only it is not fashionable. When shall we cease to prostrate ourselves before that Juggernaut of fashion? For all paces and in every instance it is better, and the risk of accidents is reduced at *least one half*. It is a wonderful ease in long rides to *vary the stirrup length*. The military, almost straight-leg, trot, I think the easiest, but, on the other hand, some of the best riders I have ever seen abroad ride with a very short stirrup; it is a matter of habit and custom. But if the fashion were once introduced here, I know it would prove a priceless boon to ladies who love riding. Let some lady who has the opportunity once try it in her own private grounds (at first) or in some quiet, out-of-the-way country lane or moorland, and she will be surprised. It is a *new existence on horseback*, and *nothing* indelicate about it, clad as I have named. Oh, what a difference it does make. It is twenty-three years now since I first took the idea from a book published by a lady, entitled, *Unprotected Females in Norway*, and whenever I can, I always ride so, of course abroad or even in the far north of Scotland. What a sensation in the Row would a party of ladies make thus mounted! Again, it is much easier for the horse, having your weight fairly distributed, not all perched on one side. Your seat is much firmer; leaping is, oh, so easy; in fact, your power seems doubled in every way. In case of conflict with your horse, you feel a veritable centaur compared with the side seat, where you have no grip, only the aid of the saddle, but with the aid of your own knees and a foot on each side of the horse I think I *could not be thrown.* Oh, I wish it could be initiated, dear Mr. Editor. Do use your influence in this direction. And it really looks well when the dress is well-made and tasty, and you feel so very free and at ease, can turn about any way, not pinned on to your horse, or rather on to your saddle, as ladies are. I could give full directions to make an outfit for going abroad in this style; you would smile at my saddle I know, but it is so comfortable. I can hardly bear to ride on an orthodox one now. That is the worst of it. I have been mounted on mules in this manner in Honduras, and ridden immense distances without being stiff or tired unduly. Some of these are the animals to try *your mettle and seat,* and I was only once thrown, owing to a stirrup-leather breaking. Then a lady is able to use spurs as easily as possible, no trouble about habit skirts tearing or getting in the way of the spur. With a sharp spur on each foot you can do anything with your horse, so very different from the wretched box spurs, eternally entangled in your habit or out of order. I do wish an association could be formed to carry out the idea; one or two could not do it, it must be simultaneous. For little girls it would be simply invaluable as an improvement on the present style, which really does cause distortion of the spine and a one-sided carriage when girls ride much. Do please ventilate this question, and oblige very much,

Yours, &c.

HERSILIE.

P.S.--I have taken your paper ever since October 2nd, when I first saw *Ladies on Horseback* in it, and have been much pleased with it, and also much amused with the correspondence thereon, but I never expected to see ladies' change of seat advocated, and am so glad to-day to find that it is.

* * * * *

SIR,--Permit me to state that the object in having the screw rowel-pin in the spur, recommended by me for the use of ladies in your number of November 13th, is in order to enable the wearers to use a mild or a severe rowel, according to the requirements of the horses they ride. I am very much against sharp spurs for ladies (or gentlemen either), unless they are absolutely required; but from some experience, both at home and abroad, I am quite convinced that the wearing of a spur should be the rule and not the exception. If the rowel is moderately sharp only, no cruelty can arise, less I maintain than in the use of a whip. I strongly object to the use of the sheath spur because of its severity; it must be applied with a *kick* to be of any use, and the effect is usually much more punishing than there is any necessity for. If ladies will use rowel spurs with *moderately* sharp rowels, such as are usual in gentlemen's park spurs, they will find that they are in possession of a very useful aid (certainly not a cruel one), and if fitted on a neat patent leather hussar or Wellington boot, a very ornamental one as well.

I am, &c.

JACK SPUR.

December, 1880.

* * * * *

SIR,--The correspondence on Mrs. Power O'Donoghue's articles has contained many remarks on ladies' spurs, but I have noticed scarcely any reference to one point which I think is worth consideration--namely, the mode of fastening. I think ladies would find it an advantage to wear what are known as "spring" or "box" spurs, instead of those fastening with the usual straps, or strap and chain. I have never seen a lady's spur of this description, but possibly they are made--if not, they easily could be. They are much the most easy to attach or remove, and there is no chance of a strap being cut in walking or otherwise, or of an over-tight buckle hurting the foot. Their principal advantage, however, is not one of mere convenience, but of safety; the absence of strap and buckle removes one element in a great danger--that of the foot sticking in the stirrup in a fall. Captain Whyte-Melville speaks from observation of the risk of the buckle catching in the angle of the stirrup-iron, and says he has never seen a spurless boot so entangled. He is arguing against the wearing of spurs at all; but the risk is avoided if box spurs be worn. Since I became convinced that the strap and buckle were a quite possible, though perhaps unlikely, source of danger, I have altogether discarded them, and have felt my feet more free in the stirrups in consequence. Box spurs are certainly not fashionable in the hunting-field, and I have often seen people looking askance at them; I suppose a particular man misses the finish that the strap gives to the boot. But I don't think that matters much, and to ladies it would not matter at all, as the difference could very seldom be detected. In getting spurs or boxes, I find it convenient to adhere always to the regulation cavalry size, because then one's old spurs fit one's new boots, and *vice versâ.* It would be well to have a uniform standard for ladies' spurs also. I have not ventured to say anything on the subject of spurs generally--my own opinion is that legitimate occasion for their use is excessively rare--and I dare say my suggestion may seem very trivial. But I do not think any precaution is trivial which lessens, however slightly, the risk of that most disagreeable and dangerous of accidents--getting "hung up."

I am, Sir,

Your obedient servant,

OXONIAN.

Ball. Col., Oxon., December, 1880.

* * * * *

SIR,--I cannot but feel flattered that my *Ladies on Horseback* papers should have called forth so large a correspondence. I have read every letter most carefully, and on perusing that of "Hersilie," which appeared in last week's issue, it struck me, from two of her observations, that persons might suppose I had said something to advocate the style of riding of which she approves. Permit me to say, emphatically, that I have never done so, and that I fervently hope, in the interests of my sex, that such a practice may never be introduced. Modesty is, in my opinion, a woman's most exquisite attribute; once this, or the semblance of it, is lost, her fairest charm is gone. Nothing could be more ungraceful or more unwomanly than for women to ride like men; and for short women or "little girls," it would be *most* objectionable. I maintain that a lady who knows how to sit has a far safer and surer seat on a side-saddle than a man can ever have, and that her grip of the pommels affords her infinitely greater security than a man's "grip of the knees." "Hersilie" is correct in saying that short-skirted hunting-habits frequently ride up, but she might just as well say that hunting-hats frequently fall off, and that ladies' back hair frequently comes down--giving these facts as a reason for discarding head-gear, whether natural or artificial. As a rule, nothing that is properly made and properly adjusted ever comes to grief. It is by going to cheap and incompetent habit-makers, neglecting to stitch elastics to their hats, and plaiting the hair too loosely (being also too sparing of hair-pins), that ladies are inconvenienced and made to blush. Two yards wide round the hem is ample for a hunting-habit, which should fit like a glove about the hips. First-class tailors always have a model horse, upon which they mount their lady customers, and thus secure the right position for the slope at the knee, upon which so much of the "set" of the skirt depends. A well-dressed woman, sitting properly upon a well-constructed saddle, cannot, in my opinion, be improved upon for style and comfort, and I hope it will be long indeed before ladies strive to follow in any way the customs or callings of the sterner sex. I may add that one of the chief recommendations of a box spur is that it does *not* get out of order, nor can it possibly become entangled, unless the habit-skirt be one of those which some ladies still persist in wearing--nearly twice too long, and quite three times too wide. I earnestly hope "Hersilie" will take these observations in good part. I make them in a perfectly friendly spirit. I feel kindly towards all ladies, especially those who love horses; and so I offer "Hersilie" a warm shake-hands, and hope she will fight me as much as ever she likes--in a friendly way, of course!

Now, a word to "Jack Spur." I think he is under a mistake in averring that there is any severity in the sheath spur. He says it must be applied with a *kick*. As I always ride with one, and never with any other description, I must entirely differ from him in this opinion. A slight pressure is alone necessary. No gentlewoman would be guilty of kicking her horse. I strongly object to rowels, as I hold to the belief that almost anybody--except a really first-class *équestrienne*--would be likely to hurt or worry the horse in an unnecessary manner.

Strange to say, I had only got thus far in my letter when the post brought me a communication from Stirling, signed "Reform," begging of me to advocate ladies riding upon the cross-saddle. Were it not that the writer says so many nice, kind things of myself (for which I beg to thank her) I should be really angry at the tremendous display of zeal thus wasted upon so unworthy a subject. It is true that a lady's seat on horseback prevents her pressing her horse up to his bridle as a man can, *unless*--but there *is* the unless--she knows how to do it. A good stout hunting-crop, properly used, will admirably fulfil the duties of the second leg; but in all my experience, and it is a pretty wide one, I have never seen more than two lady riders who had any idea of making a horse gallop or sending him up to his bit. I do not mean riding his head off--we unfortunately see too much of that; but pressing him up to his work, and riding him with firm, *accomplished* hands, such as are only to be obtained by good teaching, long and constant practice, and real love of the art. To give some idea of the hazy notion which most persons have about riding, a lady who came to call upon me in London, and who certainly meant to be most kind and polite, said, as we sat at our afternoon tea, "I am looking at your hands; how well-developed they are, from *pulling your horses*, I suppose!" She thought I was offended when I told her that my riding gloves were No. 6, and that I never pulled my horses; but I am not captious, nor would it be possible to take offence with one who so little intended to cause it.

The offer which I made at the conclusion of my *Ladies on Horseback*, to answer private inquiries, has led to such a host of letters that, although I regularly devote one hour every morning to the task of replying to each in turn, I find it impossible to keep pace with the work. Will you, therefore, sir, with the kindness extended to me upon a former occasion, suffer me to answer a few of my correspondents through the medium of your columns.

RICHARD R.--One measure three times daily, with a good double-handful of Indian corn mixed through it.

CAPTAIN SWORDARM.--The oats will require two waters. The grains should swell and separate, like rice boiled for curries.

EVELYN HARKESS.--Your parcel has not reached me. My tailor will endeavour to please you.

JANE V.--A very cruel practice.

REFORM.--You will see that I have acknowledged your letter. Judging by the postmark it should have come to hand three days ago, but you gave the wrong address, and it went on a seeking expedition. "Dublin" will at any time find me. This is also for

"Quilp," "B. Max," and "Violet Grey."

ELLA.--Your horse is evidently a rough trotter, and can never be pleasant to ride. Try to exchange or sell him.

MARY PERPLEXED.--The pommels of your saddle are most likely too far apart; that is, the leaping head is placed too low. If you cannot change it, ride with a longer stirrup-leather. I have been lately shown the preparation for an improved side-saddle, by Messrs. F. V. Nicholls & Co., of 2 Jermyn Street, comprising a patented arrangement for the third crutch or leaping-head. I think that this will be a great boon to those ladies who, like myself, have suffered inconvenience and accident from the leaping-head being a fixture, and not in the position required to afford a proper degree of support, and at the same time to admit of the stirrup-leather being used of correct length for an easy, secure, and graceful seat. The improvement of the new saddle consists in a sliding socket or apparatus, by which the leaping-head can be moved freely backward or forward to any position, and instantly fixed firmly by the rider herself, thus enabling a lady to alter at any time the length of her stirrup, and yet gain every requisite support from the third crutch. Another little innovation by the same experienced saddlers in riding bridles, an adaptation of my favourite double-ring snaffle. The loose rings of the snaffle have some extra loops, appended to which is a short noseband, acted upon by one rein, giving a powerful effect in stopping a runaway horse, whilst the use of the other rein singly has the pleasant and easy nature of the ordinary snaffle-bridle. The principle of this bridle, which is called "the improved Newmarket snaffle" is, of course, equally applicable to the use of persons of either sex.

GILES.--Have the shoe taken off and give him rest.

URSA MAJOR.--There is no real cure for ringbone. Do not waste your money.

CLAUDE, EMMA VANE, N. PARKES, HENRY B., RHODA, NELLIE K., and thirty-one others, write to me for--photographs! I am sorry that "for lack of gold" I cannot supply a kindly public with my pictures, and I am not vain enough to state publicly where they may be had.

NIMROD.--Pleader was purchased from me last week by the Earl of Eglinton. It will, therefore, be unnecessary for me to reply to any further inquiries respecting him. I named his price and made no change, nor was I asked to do so.

CROPPER.--You were evidently sitting loosely, and thus suffered for your carelessness. You will not be caught napping the next time.

ANXIOUS, MARTHA, and a host of others have asked me a very familiar question, "How I learned to ride?" I have hitherto avoided answering, rather than introduce a name whose owner did not wish me to do so. But I think I may hope to win his pardon. Most, if not all, my skill in the saddle is mainly due to the kind and untiring patience of my dear old friend and teacher, Mr. Allan McDonogh, who--despite his threescore years and ten--was, up to the time of his lamentable accident, ever ready to act as my pilot and instructor.

ENQUIRER.--Ride a steady horse, and your nerve will come back again. Mine did, after a much more terrible mischance.

CORSICAN BROTHER.--It is not true.

CRITIC.--You only discovered one mistake, but there are really *three* in my story, "In Search of a Wonder," which appeared in the Christmas Number of this journal. In place of "hustled me out *of* a sort of enclosure," read "*to* a sort of enclosure." Also, "suddenness" requires two n's, and "carr*a*ttella" is the correct way to spell a word which signifies a small cart or rough carriage peculiar to the Piedmontese. These are all printer's errors, and should have been corrected by me, but I revised my proof in a crowded coffee-room of a London hotel, with at least a dozen persons talking to me as I did so, and thus, being also pressed for time, a few mistakes escaped my notice.

To you, sir, and to all my friends, best wishes for the New Year, and many grateful thanks for more kindness than I can deem myself worthy of.

Yours obediently,

NANNIE POWER O'DONOGHUE.

Dublin, December 1880.

* * * * *

SIR,--In case no one more able than myself answers "Hersilie's" letter in this week's number of your valuable paper, will you allow me, in the name of many lady riders who "can" use the side-saddle, to write and protest against the idea cropping up of our riding like men? I cannot help feeling justly indignant with those who try to introduce such a radical change, for, surely, we are already too much inclined to follow all the ways and pursuits of the opposite sex without so far forgetting ourselves as to wish to ride as they do. I do not want to criticise what one is often obliged to do in foreign lands; there it may prove a necessity, for the riding is not simply for pleasure, but often the only means of transport, and the horses may not be fitted for our saddles, nor we accustomed to their paces; but, in England, the idea of a number of ladies fantastically dressed and mounted like men must shock many of your readers. I hope "X. Y. Z.," who first wrote in favour of this change some weeks ago, may pardon me if I say that the ladies of his or her acquaintance who, in consequence of only one stirrup, cannot avoid inclining the head and shoulders too much to the left, &c., and in addition gall their horses' backs, had better not attempt to ride at all. What is a prettier sight than a neatly-dressed Englishwoman riding a horse, "as a lady," and should we retain the same respect we now get if we gave up, in this particular, the few feminine tokens left to us. Why not let us accept the male attire altogether? It would be far more to our comfort in getting about on foot, and if one change is so advisable, surely the other is quite as sensible. I agree with "Hersilie" in thinking that the habits of the present day are indelicately short, and I cannot see that ladies ride any better showing their boots and with their arms akimbo than they did a year or so ago, when their feet were covered and no daylight showed between their arms. I come of as "horsey" a family as any in England, and have ridden ever since I could sit upright; but I never experienced, or knew that my sisters experienced, any of the troubles "X. Y. Z." and "Hersilie" complain of. My father, who was our sole instructor, put us on any animal that he thought likely to suit his own riding, and no matter where we were, in the hunting-field or elsewhere, the least deviation from sitting square would bring from him the sharp reprimand of, "What are you doing? Bring that left shoulder up, and don't let me see any daylight between your arms!" He also insisted that our stirrups should be short, even to discomfort, until we got used to it; but this prevented any chance of our hurting the horse's back, which most frequently comes from a lady riding with a long stirrup, and when she trots having to seek her stirrup, which constantly moves her saddle, and makes her as well look most awkward and one-sided.

If not trespassing too much, may I say one other little word in the interest of the horses I love so well? Over and over again, lately, have I seen the advice given in your paper that we should never be without a spur. Now, sir, if my experience can have any weight, I will say that I have hunted and ridden across country in all parts of Gloucestershire all my young days, that I was put on horses whether they or I liked it or not, both kind, unkind, or violent ones, and I am thankful to say that the idea of my wearing a spur never entered my father's head nor mine. It seems to me such an underhand way of punishing one's horse--a real feminine species of torture, for no one sees the dig, dig, dig, but there it is all the time; and many a horse, I firmly believe, comes to grief with its rider simply because, not understanding its power, she taxes it beyond its strength. Not one horse in twenty will refuse, or need either whip or spur if he knows his mistress, and if he does he is not fit for inexperienced riders.

I wish every girl was taught as I have been, "that a horse can do no wrong." This made me study the peculiarities of every animal I was put upon, and I have never had an accident of any kind. Every horsewoman who loves riding must be proud of the feats accomplished by Mrs. Power O'Donoghue in the side-saddle, but would she be admired or respected as she is if she turned out as a man and rode as men do? It is being able to sit square and ride straight on a side-saddle, that we should be vain of, and not wish to make a change, which could only bring Englishwomen down in the estimation of all those who are now so justly proud of them on horseback.

I am, Sir,

Yours, &c.

THE LADYBIRD.

December 18, 1880.

* * * * *

SIR,--Will you allow me to make one or two remarks upon a letter I read last night in your valuable paper? It is from a correspondent speaking of the ill effects produced by the use of side-saddles.

In the first place your correspondent should remember that the back of the horse, as well as the shoulder, is soft and tender when not in condition, that is, in constant work, and not fit for either riding or driving long distances at once, without damage. Get the back carefully and well seasoned, or accustomed to the side-saddle, during the time the horse is getting into condition for the hunting-field, and use a leather saddle-cloth under the saddle; let it be long enough, and not the shape of the saddle, and have all properly put on the horse, and you will not come to grief with six or seven hours' work, or before the lady is tired; that is, provided the lady will sit well down and steady in her saddle, and keep her horse as much from trotting as possible. Her horse must learn to canter slowly both to cover and home, it will be much better for the horse and much easier for the lady when she is accustomed to it; she will not be troubled any more with horses with sore backs. Another remark from "X. Y. Z." is, it is said that curvature of the spine sometimes ensues from children being taught at too early an age to ride on side-saddles. I fear the mistake is by the said children not having been taught how to sit or to put themselves in form for their own comfort, but left to sit as they like on horseback and get bad habits they cannot get rid of, never throwing the weight of the body in its proper place. Then, as to the remark about the riding-habit on the pommels, that disadvantage either has, or ought to have, passed away a long time ago; for I am well satisfied that a lady can so dress herself for the hunting-field in boots, Bedfords, and plenty of flannel that she can keep herself warm and comfortable without a great, strong, heavy, long riding-habit. Let the habit be short and very light, and by no means bound round the bottom part with anything strong, but left so that it will give way either in a fall or in leaping through a high fence. I wonder if Mr. Lovell had his knife in his pocket when he saw his daughter suspended by the habit, which would neither tear nor be removed; had it been of light, thin material, and short, the sad accident would not have occurred. I am satisfied a little care and proper attention will put all things right of which your correspondent complains.

I am, &c.

O. P.

December, 1880.

* * * * *

SIR,--In your issue of the 4th December, "Farmer" writes that his horses are fed upon oats which have been soaked in cold water, and that he has the corn thus prepared because he could not easily manage to have a steaming apparatus for cooking the food in the way that is recommended by Mr. Edward Mayhew M.R.C.V.S., in his *Illustrated Horse Management*. The plan that I have adopted during the last two months has been to have the oats put in a pail (made of oakwood) in the evening, and to pour upon them from a kettle a sufficient quantity of boiling water to rise a little above the oats; a sack is placed over it to keep in the heat, and the oats are then left to soak during the night; on the following morning the husk is so much softened that it will yield to the pressure of the thumb and finger. In this state the oats are more easily digested by the horse, and it is better for his teeth than to have to bite a hard substance. A wooden pail is preferable to a zinc one, because it does not conduct the heat from the oats so much as one of the latter description does. A lid would be, perhaps, better than a sack. The pail should not be filled with the oats, because the latter will swell when soaked. In the stall in our stable there is no water-trough at the side of the manger, and in order that the horse may have water within reach during the day and night, a zinc pail is placed in and at the end of the manger, and the handle of it is secured by a chain to the iron bars forming the upper part of the partition between the two stalls. In the loose-box, a pail containing water is suspended by a chain to some iron bars placed inside the window.

I am, &c.

X. Y. Z.

London, December, 1880.

* * * * *

SIR,--I cannot but feel flattered that Mrs. O'Donoghue has so frankly and kindly invited me to "break a lance" with her. I do, with both my hands and with all my heart, reciprocate her "warm shake-hands," and, vizor down and spear in rest, ride full tilt at her in fair and open fight to do my poor *devoirs*, if you will allow me once again to enter the lists in your paper. If Mrs. O'Donoghue will read her paper in your number for November 27th she will find these words: "My companion was in ease while I was in torture." Why was this? "Because he had a leg on either side of his mount, his weight equally distributed, and an equal support upon both sides; in fact, he had, as all male riders have, the advantage of a double support in the rise; consequently, at the moment when his weight was removed from the saddle, it was thrown upon both sides, and this equal distribution enabled him to accomplish without fatigue that slow rise and fall which is so tiring to a lady whose weight, when she is out of the saddle, is thrown entirely upon one delicate limb, thus inducing her to fall again as soon as possible."

Again, in the very next paragraph, Mrs. O'Donoghue says, "A man will be able to stand in his stirrups for a considerable time, even to ride at a gallop, so doing because he transfers his weight equally to his feet; but how rarely do we see a lady balanced upon one leg! The sensation is not agreeable, and would, moreover, be unpleasantly productive of wrung backs." These are verbatim extracts from "Part Three continued." I think my preference for a leg on each side of my horse, and a distribution of my weight equally on to each foot, is most eloquently and forcibly justified by Mrs. O'Donoghue when she wrote the above. I did not suggest, or at any rate did not mean to suggest, that she advocated a cross-seat for ladies, but that she unmistakably pointed out the great advantages of such a seat her own words abundantly testify. Again, some of the healthiest children I have ever seen are poor little gipsy girls, who, from being able to mount a donkey, have always ridden astride when once past the pannier period of their nomadic life. Also, some of the short, stout peasant women of Normandy ride thus, as well as the Indian squaws, and certainly these will compare favourably as to robust health with their side-saddle sisters of civilisation; to say nothing of the South American ladies. We have also the testimony of many lady travellers as to the superiority of a cross-seat when horseback is the only mode of transit. I cannot admit that in any case, even for "short women" or "little girls," it would be "most objectionable," that is, from a hygienic point of view. On the score of modesty, *de gustibus*, &c. &c. But then I allow a great latitude on such a point (our highest order carries the truest motto, *honi soit qui mal y pense*). In fact, I do not regard it as a question of modesty at all; simply of convenience, efficiency, and comfort. Mrs. O'Donoghue also says how rare it is to meet with a perfect lady's horse. "In all my wide experience I have met but two." Why? because a lady (and mainly on account of her side-seat, as I believe) is heavily handicapped as compared with a man in her choice of a horse, or, I should say, in her requirements from her horse. Every remark in the whole of the papers, "Ladies on Horseback," as to kindness, temper, and gentleness in the treatment of a horse I most cordially endorse, and I have to thank the fair authoress for the pleasure I have had in their perusal.

A word or two in answer to "The Ladybird." In reply to her opening remarks, I merely observe, "use is second nature," and had she happened to have lived before "Anne of Bohemia" introduced side-saddles she would have had no room for "indignation"; possibly in that case she would have always ridden pillion. Oh! if we could only once realise how much we are the slaves of fashion, how soon would the yoke be broken! Contrast the crinoline of 1857 and the umbrella-case attire of 1877; put a fashionable belle of the latter alongside her sister of only twenty years earlier mode. What a satire on taste, on modesty so called! But I would also ask "Ladybird" (if it be worth her while) to read again my letter of the 18th, and she will find I did not complain of the side-saddle, which I have an idea I *can* use, but pointed out its great inferiority (which I maintain) to the cross-saddle. The best test perhaps is the foreign one. Mount a horse without a saddle, but properly bitted, and then decide which is the more natural and easier seat; in one case you feel an appendage; in the other almost part of the horse. In the name of womanhood I repudiate the suggestion of an "underhand way of punishment," being "a real feminine species of torture." Perhaps it is, under the skirts of a habit, possible to "dig, dig, dig," for no one sees, truly; but surely no lady could, or would, spur her horse for the sake of tormenting him; in my attire at any rate it would not be unseen. The extraordinary teaching that a "horse can do no wrong" is an axiom with which I cannot agree. I have been mounted on horses that "could do no right," or if they could do it would not. And it has taken me all my time and taxed all my energies to prevent them from doing the things which they ought not to do; for I do object to a horse attempting to erect himself in a perpendicular attitude, either from a fore or aft basis, when I am on his back, and I rejoice to know that I have (in such cases) on each foot a sharp spur to use with him as a cogent argument in convincing him that ordinary progression on four legs is infinitely better than saltimbantique performance on two--at least from my, his rider's, point of view. On a well-bred, highly-trained animal a spur is scarce ever required to be used, but even then the emergency may arise. I really laughed outright when I read what you, Sir, said of the "shoals of letters" arriving from fair correspondents "desiring to ride" as "Hersilie" suggested, but this only convinces me that there are many ladies who feel that it would be--just exactly as I described it--"a new life on horseback." I could add much more on the subject, but have already trespassed too long on your space. I only repeat, let any lady once fairly try it, and she will always prefer it. I do not for a moment imagine she will always do it. I admit we must conform to custom, and I strongly deprecate individual eccentricity, especially in a lady. I shall continue to read all that appears in your paper on this and kindred topics with deep interest. Again, I specially thank Mrs. Power O'Donoghue for her genial and kindly expression of goodwill, and again heartily shake the shadowy hand she offers. I quite believe a No. 6 gloved hand can control a horse as well as any 7, 7½, or 8, if it only be possessed of the cunning. And thanking you, sir, for your kindness, allow me as a woman to have the last word, and again assert, "the cross seat is much the better."

Yours, &c.

HERSILIE.

Ambleside (*pro tem.*), Dec. 1880.

* * * * *

SIR,--Kindly permit me to say a few words in reply to "Hersilie's" letter, which appeared in your issue of last week. I am referred to my own paper in your number for November 27, but "Hersilie" does not quote correctly, or perhaps the error is the printer's. I think I said "My companion was *at* ease, whilst I was in torture." Now, I merely related the incident with which these words were associated in order to instruct ladies how to avoid the double rise--not to advocate for a single instant their riding upon a cross-saddle. I am quite ready to reiterate my statement that the position of a man enables him to ride a rough or clumsy trotter with infinitely greater ease than can a woman; but women should not, in my opinion, ride such *at all*, nor should I have done so, as related in your paper of November 27, were it not that my host, an immensely heavy man, had none but big rough horses in his stable, and I was obliged either to accept a mount upon one of them, for at least *once*, or give offence to a dear kind friend, which I would not do to avoid even a greater amount of inconvenience than I experienced upon the occasion in question.

The cross-seat is not the only thing which ladies may envy the sterner sex, without at the same time advocating the propriety of encroaching upon their privileges. For my own part I never yet set out to walk on a wet or muddy day without sincerely envying every man who passed me, his big boots, tucked-up trousers, and freedom from the petticoats and furbelows which encumber us and make us feel miserable in the rain; yet I certainly never felt the *smallest* desire to adopt his costume. Nor have I ever seen two persons, or two big dogs, engaged in fighting, that I did not envy the man who rushed between the combatants and stopped the unseemly exhibition; yet I decidedly experienced no wish to do it myself. It would not be my place. Men have their costume, their avocations, their sayings and doings, their varied callings in the world, and women have theirs. Each should be separate and distinct from the other. A manly woman, or a womanly man, is, in the eyes of all rightly-judging persons, a most objectionable creature. There are many things which a woman may legitimately admire, and, in a certain sense, *envy*, yet with which she should never desire to meddle, unless she is ambitious to merge her womanhood in the semblance of man. The cross-saddle is one of these. It may do very well in the wilds of a country whose inhabitants are from childhood accustomed to it, and where all ride alike, but not in civilised England. As well seek to advocate the dress (or undress) of the Indian squaws, as to endeavour to introduce their style of riding into a land whose daughters are as modest as they are fair.

"Hersilie" says:--"I do not regard it as a question of modesty at all, simply of convenience, efficiency, and comfort." The subject is one upon which a woman can touch but very lightly, yet may I affirm that if all women were to lay aside their chief charm, and simply go in for "convenience, efficiency, and comfort," society would present fewer attractions than it at present does? I shall leave "The Ladybird" to answer for herself, but I cannot help saying that I think "Hersilie" is *hard* upon her. She and I have met but once, yet I know that she is gentle and highborn, and worthy of nothing but the love of which her own Christian heart is composed.

You, sir, must also fight your own little battle, and tell "Hersilie" she is not to "laugh outright" at any of your "Circular Notes." She may laugh, of course, at small fry like myself, but I really *can't* have my Editor laughed at! nor my sweet "Ladybird" crushed!

And now, having said so much, I once again offer a shadowy hand to my adversary, and hope that though at present we see one another but darkly, we may yet do so "face to face," and meet as friends.

A word, with your permission, to correspondents:--

EVELYN HARKESS.--I have discovered your parcel. I thought you were sending it addressed to *me*. You shall have the contents in a few days.

FLINK.--There is never one worth buying, although unwise persons bid fast and high. Try a private source, and beware of imposition.

R. KING.--The horse is sold.

H. DUNBAR, SHAMUS O'BRIEN, W. HATFIELD, and ROSE MARIE.--Your questions are of too personal a nature. If time permits I will answer privately.

IGNORAMUS.--Dose him with aloes until he is dead sick; then put a saddle on him, with a sand-bag at either side, and ring him for an hour. I warrant he will allow a man upon his back after this, nor will he seek to dislodge him either. It is much better and more humane than the whipping and spurring which is so grievous to a sensitive looker-on.

HUGH.--Apply to Mr. Chapman, Oaklands, Cheltenham.

I. STARK.--How shall I thank you? but I know not when I can ride again. Your recipe, if effectual, would be indeed invaluable. I shall look for a purchaser for your cob.

MAY-BLOSSOM.--The nicest modern saddles have no stitching about them. Call at 2, Jermyn Street.

NIMROD II.--I have nothing that would suit you, nor do I ever sell my horses, unless under exceptional circumstances. I am, of course, flattered that so many are desirous of possessing what I have ridden, but my stable is *extremely* limited. See my reply to HUGH.

HANNAH POWELL.--I shall answer by letter.

SYNNORIX.--I said in a former letter that there was no cure for ringbone; I have since heard of one which I consider invaluable, and the lady who possesses it would sell it for a trifling sum. Apply to Mrs. Slark, Rose Cottage, Bletchley. I hope URSA MAJOR will see this reply to SYNNORIX, and will profit by my advice, which is to apply at once for the cure.

K. C., REDCAR.--I am pleased you found my system effectual, but are you sure you did not carry it out too rigorously? Few would have such courage.

JOCKEY.--An authority says Fairyhouse, and I dare say he is right, although there is a double at Punchestown--a big one--at which many a good man and true has come to signal grief. I saw a fine young racer killed there last year.

To EDITH, PAUL PRY, JANE BURKITT, CONSTANCE HAYE, and MOUSQUETAIRE, many thanks. If you write to the Editor he may perhaps give you information as to the possibility of what you ask.

Yours obediently,

NANNIE POWER O'DONOGHUE.

* * * * *

SIR,--As I learned from a recent letter from that most amiable and talented lady, Mrs. Power O'Donoghue, that her teacher has been the fine old sportsman, Allen McDonogh, I need wonder no longer at her having become the very brilliant horsewoman which undoubtedly she is. A finer or more graceful horseman than her teacher was, has never lived. Since growing years and increasing weight prevented him from riding his own horses he has brought out very many crack gentlemen riders within the past twenty years, some of them quite shining lights. Amongst some may be enumerated his great friend, Captain Tempest, 11th Hussars; Captain Prichard Rayner, 5th Dragoon Guards; Mr. Laurence, 4th Hussars; Captain, now Major, Hutton, 1st Royal Dragoons; Captain Brown, of the Royal Horse Artillery, who unfortunately was killed a few years since crossing the railway returning from a steeplechase meeting held near London; Captain Ricardo, 15th Hussars; Lieutenant-Colonel McCalmont, 7th Hussars; Captain Soames, 4th Hussars; and the ever-to-be-regretted Captain the Hon. Greville Nugent; and last, but by no means least, Mr. Thomas Beasley, besides many others, all these gentlemen, excepting Mr. Laurence, having their first winning mount on Mr. McDonogh's horses. As professionals, he brought out Paddy Gavin and George Gray, the former of whom, when scarcely more than a child, and weighing but 4 st. 7 lb., rode and won the Prince of Wales' Steeplechase, at Punchestown, on Blush Rose. I think I may be permitted to mention two of Mr. McDonogh's daring feats. When riding Sailor in a steeplechase, over an awfully severe country, close to the town of Bandon, Co. Cork (where started, amongst nine others, the celebrated horses Monarch and Valentine, the latter running second, two years later, for the Liverpool Grand National, and the former sold soon afterwards to the great Marquis of Waterford for a large sum, showing that the company at Bandon was by no means a contemptible lot), in this race, the distance of which was 4-1/2 miles, Sailor fell four times, each time unseating his rider; yet so active was his pilot in those days that he was as quickly in the saddle as out of it. At his fourth and last fall, the horse chested the bank, flung his rider some distance from him, and having a tight hold of the bridle reins, the throat-lash gave way, and the bridle came off the horse's head. As Sailor was getting on his legs, Mr. McDonogh jumped into the saddle, and setting his horse going was soon in pursuit of the leaders. There were in the 1-1/2 miles that had yet to be travelled nearly ten awkward double-posted fences. The third last impediment was a narrow lane--called in Irish a "boreen"--with an intricate bank into and out of it. The riders of Valentine and Monarch had bridles; consequently they could steady their horses and jump in and out "clever." Not so Mr. McDonogh, who had nothing to guide his horse but his whip. Steering the animal, however, for the "boreen" he put him at his best pace, and without ever laying an iron on it, he went from field to field and landed alongside the leaders. The riders of the other horses, seeing he had no power to guide his mount, endeavoured to put him outside a post that had to be gone round to make the turn into the straight line for home; but the young jockey, stretching his arms almost round his horse's nose, by some means got him straight, and, making the remainder of the running, won easily. Valentine's rider at the scales objected to Sailor for not having carried a bridle, but Mr. McDonogh was able to draw the weight, and was declared the winner amidst the wildest enthusiasm. The other extraordinary performance occurred one day on his pet mount, the celebrated Brunette, at Cashel. When riding Mountain Hare the previous day over the same course he was crossed by an old woman at an ugly up bank. The horse struck the woman in the chest and very nearly put an end to his rider also, who, in the fall, got his collar-bone and six ribs broken. The late Dr. Russell, of Cashel, was quickly by his side, and telling the Marquis of Waterford of the serious injuries Mr. McDonogh had received, that most noble-hearted man instantly sent for his carriage, which, with two post-horses, speedily took the invalid to the hotel in Cashel. The collarbone being set and ribs bandaged, he passed a miserable night. Brunette was in a race the next day, and as he would allow no man to sit on her back, he got out of his bed, mounted the mare, and, bandaged as he was and in great pain, won the race. Lord Waterford's Regalia was second, his lordship jestingly remarking that if he had known Brunette's master would have ridden her he would have left him lying at the bank, In conclusion, Mr. Editor, permit me to say that we Irish are charmed with Mrs. O'Donoghue's writings, as also with your most interesting and beautifully got-up paper.

Yours, &c.

MAURICE LAWLOR.

Battlemount, Ballytore, Co. Kildare.

* * * * *

SIR,--Notwithstanding the enterprise of the large number of ladies who, you say, desire to ride after the fashion of the Mexican senoras, I venture to hope that the present custom of riding in a side-saddle will not be departed from by ladies, except in case of necessity; and I point out that in India, South Africa, and all the Australian colonies the side-saddle is always used, though there can be no doubt that if there was any real advantage in the Mexican style it would be readily adopted in new countries. Many persons appear to be quite unaware of what the lady's seat in the side-saddle should be. I describe it thus: let a man seat himself properly in his saddle, shorten the left stirrup two or three holes, and then, without moving his body or his left leg, put his right leg over the horse's wither; the man will then be seated on his horse precisely as a lady should be seated in her side-saddle. A lady's seat in a side-saddle, of the size suited to her, is extremely firm; any one who has not tried a side-saddle with the third crutch has no idea of the firm seat that a lady has. I was quite astonished when I tried it, and I believe that, after practising for a day or two to get the balance, I could ride any horse in a side-saddle that I could ride at all; whilst the exploits of ladies show clearly that a change of style is not required for the purpose of obtaining a more secure seat. One of the greatest difficulties that ladies have to contend with in this country in learning to ride is that they often get such poor instructors. Many of those who call themselves riding masters are little better than grooms, and the people who offer to turn out accomplished horsewomen in twelve easy lessons for £2 2s. must know that, except in a few cases of natural special aptitude, they cannot do much more than teach a lady how to avoid tumbling too quickly out of the saddle. On the other hand, a lady who has been through a full course of instruction from a good master, has little to learn except those matters of detail which experience alone can teach; but far better than any professional instruction is that constant and careful supervision from a good horseman, such as Mrs. Power O'Donoghue and "The Ladybird" mentioned in a late issue, one who will not be afraid of being called a "bother" when he points out and corrects every fault, however small. I consider, sir, that you have given good advice to ladies when you say, "I think a lady should wear a spur," though she may not often find it necessary to use it. In your last issue two experienced ladies give their opinions on this subject; one disapproves of the spur, the other says she always wears one. Everyone will agree with "The Ladybird" that when it is "dig, dig, dig" all the time, such use of a spur is improper; for though a sharp stroke is required sometimes--for instance, Mrs. Power

O'Donoghue, when describing her flight into the farmyard, says: "I dug him with my spur"--the proper way to apply a spur is, in general, as described by Mrs. Power O'Donoghue in your last issue, by pressure. The term "box spur" is usually applied to spurs that fit into spring boxes or sockets in the heels of the boots; a spur with a spring sheath over the point is usually called a "sheath spur"; for hunting, anything that will act as a goad will answer the desired purpose, but for park or road riding the spur should be one with which a very slight touch or a sharp stroke can be given, as may be required. I know that the spur with a five-pointed rowel is preferred by ladies who have tried it to any other; but, whatever spur is selected, a lady should take care that the points are long enough to be effective when the habit intervenes. I think, sir, with you, that a lady should always wear a spur; and I notice in this correspondence, the ladies who denounce the use of a spur almost invariably say that they have never tried one; whilst ladies who have once experienced the advantage and convenience of it, never willingly mount a horse without one. There is not any real mystery about ladies' riding or ladies' horses; almost any horse that will carry a man will carry a woman, and the latter, when on horseback, ought to be provided, as nearly as possible, with the same aids and appliances as are required by the former. It is not every lady who can indulge in the luxury of a three-hundred-guinea saddle-horse, and the treatment that may answer with such a horse is not necessarily suited to an ordinary hack; yet some of the handsomest and most highly-trained ladies' horses in the Row are ridden with a spur, and it is only proper that they should be; they have been trained by the professional lady riders with a spur, and they are accustomed to receive from a slight touch of the spur the indications of the rider's wish; whilst as to the common livery-stable hacks, it is often painful to ride them until they feel that you are provided with spurs, when their whole nature appears to change, and you can enjoy a tolerably pleasant ride. "The Ladybird" says she was taught "that a horse can do no wrong." As a matter of theory the idea is a very pretty one, but I can only say, as a simple matter of fact, that I have often known a horse exhibit a very large amount of what the late Mr. Artemus Ward called "cussedness"; and I know of nothing that, when a horse is in that frame of mind, will bring him to his senses so quickly, so effectually, and with so much convenience to the rider, as a sharp spur. In far-off lands, I was once nearly two hours doing a distance of some seven miles on a new purchase. I was then without spurs; but the next day, when I was provided with them, the same animal did the same distance easily and pleasantly in about forty minutes. I very much dislike to see a lady use a whip to her horse: and, as I have always proved spurs to be a great convenience, I recommend a lady to wear one, and to use it *when necessary* in preference to the whip.

I am, &c.

SOUTHERN CROSS.

December, 1880.

* * * * *

SIR,--Since I have come to London I have been asked so many questions respecting the reason why ladies so often "pull their horses," that I feel I may accomplish some good by answering, or may at least assist in doing away with a very crying evil. My opinion is that there is usually but one reason, viz. because the horses pull them; but for a woman to pull against a pulling horse only increases the evil. It is a fallacy, and can never accomplish the desired end. A determined puller cannot, under any circumstances, be suitable to a lady, and should never be ridden by one, unless she be a sufficiently good rider and have sufficiently good hands to make the horse's mouth, which is not the case with one woman in five hundred, or, I might almost say, one man either. Horses that pull have been almost invariably spoilt in the training. Occasionally a fine-mouthed animal will be ruined by an ignorant or cruel rider, but I must say, in justice to my sex, that they are seldom guilty of doing it. The fault lies amongst men. Many women are ignorant riders; but, thank God! the blot of cruelty rarely defaces their name. Women are naturally gentle, kindly, and--*cowardly*; three things calculated not to injure a horse, except it be the latter, which enables him to discover that he can be master if he please. Doubtless there are cruel women, also, who cut and lash, and tug and spur, and treat heaven's noble gifts as though they were mere machinery, and not flesh and blood like ourselves; but how often shall I say, in answer to the numerous cases cited to me, that in writing upon this or any other subject I speak of the rule, not of the isolated exceptions. When a man begins to break a horse he regularly prepares for combat. He sets himself to work with a resolute determination to fight and be fought, as though he had a strong rebellious spirit to deal with and conquer, instead of a loving, kindly, timid nature, which needs nought save gentleness to make it amenable to even the rudest hand. The man begins by pulling; the horse, on the schoolboy "tit for tat" principle, pulls against him in return; is sold before his education (bad as it has been) is half completed; is ridden out to exercise by grooms with heavy iron hands; is handed over to the riding-school and to carry young ladies when every bit of spirit has been knocked out of him, except the determined one of pulling--pulls resolutely against the feeble hands striving to control him; is pulled and strained at in return, and becomes in time a confirmed and unmanageable brute. I wish I could persuade ladies *not* to pull their horses. In a former number I endeavoured to tell them the proper method of managing or dealing with a pulling animal: neither to drop their hands to him, nor to pull one ounce against him. He will be certain after a few strides to yield a bit, when the hands--hitherto firm, should immediately yield to him, thus establishing a sort of give and take principle, which will soon be perfectly understood by the intelligent creature under control. We do not half appreciate our horses. Every touch of our fingers, every word we utter, every glance from our eye is noted by the horse, and is valued or resented as it deserves. So many animals are made unruly by the undue use of a severe curb that I strongly advise a trial of the snaffle only, holding the curb-rein loosely over the little finger, so that it may be in an instant taken up in case it prove necessary, which, in my opinion, it rarely will. To illustrate my meaning, on Monday last I rode a mare for a lady, who was very desirous of ascertaining whether the animal was capable of carrying a lady with safety. The groom, who was to accompany me, was evidently extremely nervous. He told me, as we started, that the mare had never done any saddle work, except with a very wild young gentleman-rider, who had bitted her severely, and yet found her difficult to manage; and he implored me earnestly to keep a good hold of the curb. I found that she hung desperately upon her bridle, kept her head between her knees with a strong, determined, heavy pull upon the bit, and rough, jerky action, which was most unpleasant. When I got her into the Row she nearly pulled my arms out in her canter--the tug she had upon the bridle was quite terrific; and, evidently prepared for the accustomed fight, she put back her ears and shook her wicked head angrily. I rode her from Palace Gate to Hyde Park Corner in the same manner as I have sought to impress upon my lady readers--namely, not pulling one atom against her, but keeping my hands low and firm, and yielding slightly to her in her stride. By the time we had turned at the Corner she had quite given up fighting. I then dropped the curb, and rode her entirely upon the snaffle. The effect was magical. She lifted her head, ceased pulling altogether, and went along in a pleasant joyous canter, going well up to her bridle, but not attempting any liberties whatever, In an hour's time, as you, sir, who were riding with me will bear testimony, I was holding her with *one hand*, stooping forward, and making much of her with the other, an attention which she evidently regarded as a pleasing novelty, and highly appreciated. Finding her slightly untractable during the ride homeward I once more lightly took up the curb. It maddened her in a moment. She turned round and round, ran me against a cart, and behaved so excitedly that it required my best skill, confidence, and temper to restore her equanimity and steer her safely (using the snaffle only) to her destination. On dismounting I observed to the groom that considering the amount of exercise and excitement through which she had passed, it was wonderful she had not sweated. His answer was that she was always fed upon cooked food, and that the chief sustenance of the horse which he himself was riding--a remarkably fine three-year-old--was boiled barley. I have never, myself, tried this feeding, but if looks and condition may be regarded as recommendation, it must be most excellent.

I am, Sir,

Yours obediently,

NANNIE POWER O'DONOGHUE.

* * * * *

SIR,--I have been very greatly interested by the remarks on saddles, spurs, &c., made by your lady correspondents. My husband is a large ranchero, or cattle-farmer, on the Rio Grande, between Mexico and Texas, and naturally I have had much experience of hard as well as long-distance riding. Having been accustomed to hunting when I was a girl, I came out here with an exaggerated idea of my skill in horsemanship. My first ride in Mexico was one of three hundred miles, which we did in seven days; I rode on an English hunting-saddle almost, if not quite, as "straight as a board." After the second day I found it as uncomfortable a seat as could be desired, and was glad to change it for the peon's ordinary Mexican saddle, which I found perfectly easy and comparatively comfortable to my English one. This last I have found exceedingly fatiguing and ill-adapted to a long journey, although very good for a few hours' ride after wild cattle, which is a certain approach to hunting, although the jumping is not stiff. Lately I had another saddle sent out from

England, which was a little deeper, and I find it much more useful for long distances. As ladies are not in the habit of riding steeplechases, I would venture to suggest that, for hard riding, such as hunting, the saddle might rather be heavier than lighter, as I am sure that this must give more relief to the horse's back. In fact, I believe that the sore backs so often produced by ladies' saddles are more frequently caused by the saddle being too light than too heavy. I quite agree with some of your correspondents that the padded stirrup is most dangerous, as it is not easy to get the foot out quickly if anything should happen.

The principle, as stated by the Mexicans, of striking a horse between the ears is not to bring him down by *fright*, but to bring him down by *force*, so as to "stun" him. Now, do you think that any of your fair correspondents could accomplish this with a light park or hunting-whip? I may be very bold to offer any suggestions, but the lady's sidesaddle of the nineteenth century is very far from being pleasant. Why should not ladies in this age of progression begin to ride on saddles shaped like a man's, with the same seat a man uses? It would be much more comfortable, as even a stout lady could not look much more ungraceful than she does now, besides materially lessening the danger. I send you a sketch of a Mexican saddle.

I am, &c.

CAMPESINA.

San Antonio de Bexar, Texas, U.S.A.

P.S.--I would not like you to imagine that I intend to slight such an admirable authority as Mrs. Power O'Donoghue, but I should be much obliged to any of your correspondents for the design of an improved saddle, suitable alike for riding a young nervous horse and for journey purposes. I have a design for such a saddle, but I do not know how far it may be practicable. I think if ladies would give their ideas upon this subject through the medium of your columns, some real improvement might be arrived at.

C.

* * * * *

Sir,--In your issue of the 27th November my letter appeared, recommending that the use of side-saddles should be discontinued. Your correspondent, "Jack Spur," mentions, in a letter published on the 13th November, that in some works concerning the Sandwich Islands, in the Northern Pacific Ocean, and the Rocky Mountains, North America, the authoress, Miss Isabella L. Bird, states that she was accustomed, while there, to ride on horseback astride.

A few extracts from her above-mentioned writings will probably interest your readers. When in Hawaii, or Owyhee, one of the Sandwich Islands, the authoress referred to accompanied some friends on horseback to the Anuenue Falls on the Wailuku river (a river which forms a boundary between two great volcanoes), and on that occasion used a side-saddle, but was afterwards advised by one of the party to follow the native fashion of riding astride. Having acted upon this advice, she was well satisfied with the result of the trial, and continued to adopt that style while in the Sandwich Islands, and also in the Rocky Mountains, where she remained nearly four months. The following extract from a letter written by her about the 28th of January, from Hilo, Hawaii, and published in *The Hawaiian Archipelago: Six Months in the Sandwich Islands*, 1875, page 66, gives further particulars of her visit to the Anuenue Falls, above referred to:--

"Everything was new and interesting, but the ride was spoiled by my insecure seat in my saddle, and the increased pain in my spine which riding produced. Once, in crossing a stream, the horses had to make a sort of downward jump from a rock, and I slipped round my horse's neck; indeed, on the way back I felt that on the ground of health I must give up the volcano, as I would never consent to be carried to it, like Lady Franklin, in a litter. When we returned, Mr. Severance suggested that it would be much better for me to follow the Hawaiian fashion, and ride astride, and put his saddle on the horse. It was only my strong desire to see the volcano which made me consent to a mode of riding against which I have so strong a prejudice; but the result of the experiment is that I shall visit Kilanea thus or not at all. The native women all ride astride on ordinary occasions in the full sacks, or holukus, and on gala days in the pan, the gay winged dress which I described in writing from Honolulu. A great many of the foreign ladies in Hawaii have adopted the Mexican saddle also" (this means that they ride astride) "for greater security to themselves and ease to their horses on the steep and perilous bridle-tracks, but they wear full Turkish trousers, and jauntily-made dresses reaching to the ankles."

After leaving the Sandwich Islands she went to the Rocky Mountains, and in a letter dated the 23rd of October, and published in *A Lady's Life in the Rocky Mountains*, 1879, she writes from the Colorado District, North America:--

"I rode sidewise till I was well through the town, long enough to produce a severe pain in my spine, which was not relieved for some time even after I had changed my position. It was a lovely Indian summer day, so warm that the snow on the ground looked an incongruity."

From the fact that many ladies, when in the Sandwich Islands, ride astride, and that Miss Bird found this position preferable in many respects to that which a side-saddle obliges the rider to take, I infer that ladies in England would be pleased if a change in the mode of riding were introduced.

Proprietors of circuses will perhaps permit me to offer for their consideration that by allowing this mode of riding to form a part of some of the circus performances, they might do a great deal towards causing it to be recognised by the public as the correct style, and that one great obstacle in the way of its being generally adopted by horsewomen would then be removed.

I wish also to suggest that it should be taught at several riding-schools, so that a large number of pupils may commence at the same time.

I am, Sir,

Your obedient servant,

X. Y. Z.

* * * * *

SIR,--The letters of your correspondent, Mrs. Power O'Donoghue, are very instructive and trustworthy, because founded upon practical experience. In her letter of last week she recommends the feeding of hunters upon *cooked food*. This to many sportsmen will be a new theory; not so to me, and I wish to confirm her views, but I carry them out in a more economical way. My establishment is but a small one. I cannot afford space or attendance for a cooking-house, but I believe I arrive at the same results as she does, by steeping my oats in cold water for a given number of hours, and adding a pound of Indian meal, with a handful of chopped hay and oaten straw to each feed three times a day. My horses have a constant supply of water in a manger in a convenient corner of their stables. I believe horses fed upon dry oats and hay suffer much from thirst. I observe my horses take many sups of water through the day, but take much less on the whole than when watered upon the old practice twice daily. Practically, I find my horses very healthy, strong, and enduring, and I would freely recommend the adoption of this mode of feeding hunters to my sporting friends.

FARMER.

* * * * *

SIR,--I am still so inundated with correspondence--many writers asking me precisely the same questions--that I shall regard it as a favour if you will again allow me to answer a few of them through the medium of your paper.

CONN. DASHPUR.--You and your horse were immersed in the river, simply because you did not give him sufficient head-room to enable him to take the jump with safety. In coming up to a wide stretch of water you should always leave your mount abundant opportunity to extend his head and neck, nor should you wait to do this until you are just on the brink,--it will then, most likely, be too late to save you and him a wetting. A horse stretches his neck coming up to a water-jump, partly that he may see well what is before him, and partly because his intelligence tells him that he cannot compass it if tightly reined in. Leave him his head, and if he is a hunter worth riding he will calculate his distance and bear you safely over. At the same time you must remember to give him sufficient support when he lands, or he may peck, or roll, and give you an ugly fall. A horse is much more liable to come down over a water-jump than at a fence, for the swinging pace at which you must necessarily send him at it--combined with the *absolute* necessity for leaving him complete freedom of his head--forbids that "steadying" process, which, at the hands of an accomplished rider, usually ensures safety over wall or ditch. Questions similar to yours have been asked me by H. CADLICOTT, MAURICE HONE, and GUY. In answering one, therefore, I reply to each.

ELLICE GREENWAY.--Your MS. never reached me; you must have misdirected it,--but in any case I could not have been of service to you, as I have no time for revising other people's work, nor would my recommendation carry any weight. Publishers judge for themselves. Your papers must go in on their merits, and be accepted or rejected accordingly. I quite agree with you that declined MSS. should--when accompanied by a stamped and addressed envelope--be returned to the sender with the least possible delay. No matter how great or hurried may be the business of an office, there is in reality no excuse for inattention to this rule. The very best and busiest of the weekly journals comply with it, and persons who do not want to be treated with snobbish indifference had better not write for any other. Perhaps if you call, or send a line privately to the Editor, you may succeed in getting back your work; but do not be expectant.

KING LEAR.--The horse you name attained his victory in 1878. He carried 12 st. 7 lbs.

G. HUNT.--Beauparc; but he did not win.

P. RYALL.--At Thirsk. He fell at the second obstacle, and although speedily remounted, his chance was extinguished. Pinnace ran well, and was in great form. His defeat was a surprise, but your informant has not given you reliable details.

JAMES.--Read *Silk and Scarlet*, one of the "Druid" series. Thanks for too flattering opinion.

FORDHAM.--The course is a most trying one, and the feat was one never before attempted by a lady. I did it to show that my horse was capable of accomplishing the task, and the risk was not what you describe it, for he was too clever to put a foot astray. Major Stone of the 80th accompanied me, and gave me a good lead. The only time I passed him was when his horse refused at an ugly post and rail. It is not true that he was thrown.

He rode splendidly, managing a difficult horse. There was no "crowd," and in short it is evident that you have received an exaggerated account of the affair.

J. DUNNE.--He won at Newcastle in 1879.

COLLINS W.--She was, in my opinion, unfairly handicapped, and the verdict was general respecting the matter.

DOUGLAS.--The horse was not shot for five hours after, and lay quivering all that time. The owner was absent, and four of us galloped in search of him. Nobody was to blame. Mr. W. B. Morris, 7th Hussars, was the rider, and no better ever wore silk.

MONTAUBAN.--I have already detailed at some length my objections to children riding before they have strength and judgment sufficient to enable them to manage a horse. Moreover, if a child--say a little girl--gets a severe fall, the shock to her nervous system is most likely to be a lasting one, and in some cases is never got over; whereas grown girls are less liable to fall, if they have any sort of fair teaching, and certainly have stronger nerves and firmer resolution to enable them to bear the casualties attendant upon the practice of the art.

CURIOUS.--Griffin and Hawkes, of Birmingham, by the burning of whose premises some of my most valued MSS. were lost.

JESSICA.--It is quite untrue. Her Imperial Majesty dresses and mounts in ordinary fashion. There is not one word of truth in the widely-circulated statement that her habit is buttoned on after she has mounted, nor is her jacket ever made "tight." It is close-fitting and beautifully adapted to her figure, but sufficiently large to leave her abundant room to move in. The Empress despises tight stays, gloves, and boots. Her waist is small, but not wasp-like. The absurd announcement that it measured but twelve inches (recently published in one of the weekly journals) is as false as it is foolish. Nobody could exist with such a deformity. The Empress takes morning exercise upon a trapeze. Her hair is dark, shaded to gold-colour, like a wood in autumn. The report that she dyes it is one of the many calumnies of which she is the subject, but which happily cannot harm her. She is *not* affable; her manner is stately in the extreme, to all except those with whom she desires to converse. She speaks fair but not fluent English. This reply to JESSICA is also for FRANK KURTZ, AMY ROBSART, and ALICIA BOND.

JULIUS.--It was not I who wrote it. I got the credit of it, but did not covet the distinction.

GEORGE K.--Nobody assists me. Of course you mean as an amanuensis: otherwise your question would be an offence. I write my thoughts in short-hand, and copy at leisure for the press. My time for writing is when the house is quiet,--generally from 10 P.M. to 2 or 3 in the morning. I have answered you--but against my will, as I much dislike personal questions. Were I to reply to such in general, my entire life would be laid bare to the eyes of a disinterested public, in order to gratify a few persons, who have no motive save one of idle curiosity.

T. CANNON.--*Grandfather's Hunter* is sold out. *Horses and Horsemen* is to be had, but its price puts it beyond the pale of ordinary purchasers. Try Bumpus, or Mudie.

OXONIAN.--You are wrong,--nor have I asked your opinion. It is easier to criticise than to write. Having done the former, pray do the latter, and submit to others' criticism.

MARCIA FLOOD.--Two yards round the hem is amply sufficient width. I consider the price you name quite exorbitant. Try one of those mentioned by me in my chapter upon riding-gear.

Thanking you, Sir, for your kindness in granting me so much of your valuable space.

I am, yours obediently,

NANNIE POWER O'DONOGHUE.

* * * * *

SIR,--In a recent edition "Jack Spur" asks if it is usual in any country for ladies to ride *à la* Duchess de Berri, *i.e.* as a gentleman, astride. In Mexico and the States of the River Plate this is the usual mount of the fair ones of the district, and, clad in loose Turkish pantalettes tucked into the riding-boots of soft yellow leather, a loose sort of tunic secured by a belt, and wearing the *ladies'* "sombrero," very charming these fair *équestriennes* look, and splendid horsewomen they are. Talk of ladies, your "Fair Play" should see the long, sharp, Mexican spurs attached to the heels of these fair prairie-rangers, and witness how unsparingly they are used. Sometimes I, who am no namby-pamby rider, and have seen my share of rough work, have ventured to remonstrate in a half-jocular manner (as became a stranger and foreigner) when riding along with a Mexican lady, who generally keeps her steed at a full gallop by the remorseless application of these instruments of punishment. But the reply was merely a silvery laugh, and "Ah, senor, here horses are cheap, and when one is finished we have plenty more for the catching. Come along!" My experience of ladies on horseback as a rule is that they are more severe than men; perhaps it is thoughtlessness, but certainly for hard riding and severe spurring I have never seen any to surpass a Mexican senora, whose favourite pace is a stretching gallop without cessation, until her steed is perfectly pumped out, and as horseflesh is of no value whatever, and no Society for the Prevention of Cruelty to Animals exists, I am afraid I must record a verdict of cruelty against some of the most charming women I ever met. To their fellow mortals all kindness and goodness, but when mounted on their mustang they seem to forget that he can feel either fatigue or pain. Certainly the temptation is great. A horse is of no value; you seldom mount the same twice on a journey, and across the beautiful prairies a wild gallop is the pace. But I should be sorry to see an English lady dismount from her steed, leaving him utterly exhausted and pumped out, and his flanks streaming with blood from deep spur-strokes. This I have too often seen in South America. Everyone does it, and it is little thought of; but by all means let us cherish a better feeling, and not give any needless pain to that noble animal, the horse. Let the ladies avoid the use of sharp spurs; most horses ridden by ladies here are perfectly amenable to the whip and rein, and the use of the spur is somewhat inharmonious with the gentle character of our English women.

GUACHO.

St. Leonards, 1880.

* * * * *

"The correspondence upon this subject, called forth by Mrs. Power O'Donoghue's admirable papers 'Ladies on Horseback,' has been so voluminous, and appears likely to go on for such a lengthened period, that I am reluctantly obliged to bring it to a close, in order to make space for other matter."--ED. *Illustrated Sporting and Dramatic News.*

London: Printed by W. H. Allen & Co., 13, Waterloo Place, S.W.

WORKS PUBLISHED

BY

W. H. ALLEN & CO.

HOW TO RIDE AND SCHOOL A HORSE, With a System of Horse Gymnastics. BY EDWARD L. ANDERSON. Crown 8vo. 2s. 6d.

* * * * *

MAYHEW (EDWARD) ILLUSTRATED HORSE DOCTOR. Being an Accurate and Detailed Account, accompanied by more than 400 Pictorial Representations, characteristic of the various Diseases to which the Equine Race are subjected; together with the latest Mode of Treatment, and all the requisite Prescriptions written in Plain English. BY EDWARD MAYHEW, M.R.C.V.S. 8vo. 18s. 6d.

CONTENTS.--The Brain and Nervous System.--The Eyes.--The Mouth.--The Nostrils.--The Throat.--The Chest and its contents.--The Stomach, Liver, &c.--The Abdomen.--The Urinary Organs.--The Skin.--Specific Diseases.--Limbs.--The Feet.--Injuries.--Operations.

"The book contains nearly 600 pages of valuable matter, which reflects great credit on its author, and, owing to its practical details, the result of deep scientific research, deserves a place in the library of medical, veterinary, and non-professional readers."--*Field.*

"The book furnishes at once the bane and the antidote, as the drawings show the horse not only suffering from every kind of disease, but in the different stages of it, while the alphabetical summary at the end gives the cause, symptoms, and treatment of each."--*Illustrated London News.*

MAYHEW (EDWARD) ILLUSTRATED HORSE MANAGEMENT.--Containing descriptive remarks upon Anatomy, Medicine, Shoeing, Teeth, Food, Vices, Stables; likewise a plain account of the situation, nature, and value of the various points; together with comments on grooms, dealers, breeders, breakers, and trainers; Embellished with more than 400 engravings from original designs made expressly for this work. By E. MAYHEW. A new Edition, revised and improved by J. I. LUPTON, M.R.C.V.S. 8vo. 12s.

CONTENTS.--The body of the horse anatomically considered. PHYSIC.--The mode of administering it, and minor operations. SHOEING.--Its origin, its uses, and its varieties. THE TEETH.--Their natural growth, and the abuses to which they are liable. FOOD.--The fittest time for feeding, and the kind of food which the horse naturally consumes. The evils which are occasioned by modern stables. The faults inseparable from stables. The so-called "incapacitating vices," which are the results of injury or of disease. Stables as they should be. GROOMS.--Their prejudices, their injuries, and their duties. POINTS.--Their relative importance, and where to look for their development. BREEDING.--Its inconsistencies and its disappointments. BREAKING AND TRAINING.--Their errors and their results.

* * * * *

DAUMAS (E.) HORSES OF THE SAHARA, AND THE MANNERS OF THE DESERT. By E. DAUMAS, General of the Division Commanding at Bordeaux, Senator, &c. &c. With Commentaries by the Emir Abd-el-Kadir (Authorized Edition). 8vo. 6s.

"We have rarely read a work giving a more picturesque and, at the same time, practical account of the manners and customs of a people, than this book on the Arabs and their horses."--*Edinburgh Courant.*

THURSTON & CO.

BILLIARD TABLE MANUFACTURERS.

LAMP MAKERS AND GAS FITTERS.

BY APPOINTMENT TO HER MAJESTY THE QUEEN, AND HER ROYAL HIGHNESS THE PRINCESS OF WALES.

ESTABLISHED A.D. 1814.

16, CATHERINE STREET, STRAND, LONDON.

PRIZE MEDAL, SYDNEY, 1879, FIRST AWARD.

S. & H. HARRIS'S

57, MANSELL STREET, E.,

EBONITE WATERPROOF BLACKING

FOR HUNTING OR WALKING BOOTS.

REQUIRES NO BRUSHING.

HARNESS COMPOSITION (Waterproof).

SADDLE PASTE (Waterproof).

JET BLACK OIL, For Harness.

BLACK DYE, FOR STAINING HARNESS, And all kinds of Leather.

WATERPROOF DUBBIN, For Boots and Harness.

BREECHES POWDER, For Cleaning Hunting Breeches.

LONDON, W.

WHIPS OF EVERY DESCRIPTION FOR RIDING, DRIVING, & HUNTING, &c.

WHIPS MOUNTED IN GOLD AND SILVER, FOR PRESENTATION, ALWAYS ON HAND.

HUNTING FLASKS, HORNS, &c.

THE NEW LEVEL-SEAT SIDE SADDLE,

WITH ADJUSTABLE THIRD CRUTCH AND OTHER IMPROVEMENTS,

As recommended and used by Mrs. Power O'Donoghue, Authoress of "LADIES ON HORSEBACK," &c. &c.

This perfect Side Saddle is moderate in price, light and elegant in appearance, faultless in materials and workmanship, ensures ease, comfort, and security to the rider, and obviates sore backs with horses.

MADE TO ORDER AND MEASURE BY

F. V. NICHOLLS & CO.,

HUNTING & MILITARY SADDLERS,

Manufacturers of Harness, Horse Clothing, Whips, and Stable Requisites,

2, JERMYN STREET, HAYMARKET,

LONDON.

The Gentleman's narrow-grip "Brough" Saddle, any size and weight, from £7, complete.

The Gentleman Rider's Racing Saddle, £3 to £4, complete, very roomy, with Buckskin Flaps, &c.

THE IMPROVED NEWMARKET & ING GUY SNAFFLE BRIDLES, FOR PULLING HORSES.

Branch Business: 18, ARTILLERY PLACE, WOOLWICH.

ROWLANDS' ODONTO OR PEARL DENTIFRICE

has been celebrated for more than half a century as the best, purest, and most fragrant preparation for the teeth ever made. Health depends in a great measure upon the soundness of the teeth, and all dentists will allow that neither washes nor pastes can possibly be as efficacious for polishing the teeth and keeping them sound and white as a pure and non-gritty tooth-powder; such Rowlands' Odonto has always proved itself to be. Great care must be taken to ask for ROWLANDS' ODONTO, of 20, Hatton Garden, London, and to see that each box bears the 3d. Government Stamp, without which no ODONTO is genuine.

ROWLANDS' MACASSAR OIL

is universally in high repute for its unprecedented success during the last 80 years in promoting the growth, restoring, improving, and beautifying the human hair. For children it is especially recommended, as forming the basis of a beautiful head of hair, while its introduction into the nursery of Royalty is a sufficient proof of its merits. It is perfectly free from any lead, mineral, or poisonous ingredients.

ROWLANDS' KALYDOR

produces a beautiful pure and healthy complexion, eradicates freckles, tan, prickly heat, sunburn, &c., and is most cooling and refreshing to the face, hands, and arms during hot weather.

Ask any Perfumery dealer for ROWLANDS' Articles, of 20, Hatton Garden, London, and avoid spurious worthless imitations.

MESSRS. JAY

Have the honour to solicit a visit from the Beau Monde to inspect a variety of Elegant Silk Costumes, Mantles, Artistic Millinery, Hats, also Novelties in Dress, specially selected in Paris from the best Artistes representing the Fashions of the Season.

243, 245, 247, 249, 251, & 253, Regent Street, W.

W. FAULKNER,

LADIES' & GENTLEMEN'S HUNTING, SHOOTING, & WALKING BOOT MAKER,

52, SOUTH MOLTON STREET, BOND STREET, W.

Manufacturer of the Celebrated Edinburgh Boot Varnish, Blacking, and Waterproof Leather Dressing.

MILITARY BOOTS.

The "Bective" Boots and Shoes to match Costumes.

Improved Flexura Boots.

Mountain Boots.

Skating Boots.

[Illustration: A Boot]

Lawn Tennis Shoes.

Oxford Shoes.

Slippers to any style.

LADIES' RIDING & HUNTING BOOTS OF EVERY DESCRIPTION.

The Shape of the Feet taken and Lasts Modelled on the most approved, anatomical principles, and kept exclusively for each customer.

W. FAULKNER begs most respectfully to call the attention of Ladies and Gentlemen to the BOOT TREE Branch. Boot Trees assist to keep the boots in proper shape, preventing them from wrinkling and shrinking after they have been worn in the wet; they can be cleaned better, and do not require so much blacking, thereby preventing the deleterious effect produced by its frequent application.

Lasts and Boot Trees of every description Manufactured on the Premises.

Ladies residing in the Country can have Boots or Boot Trees sent their exact size by forwarding an Old Boot by Post.

To H.R.H. PRINCESS CHRISTIAN.

SYKES, JOSEPHINE, & CO.

"CORSETS."

280, REGENT STREET, LONDON,

AND

56A, OLD STEYNE, BRIGHTON.

RIDING CORSETS OF EVERY DESCRIPTION MADE TO ORDER.

MANUFACTORIES {RUE RAMBUTEAU, PARIS. {GREAT CASTLE STREET, LONDON.

HOW TO RIDE AND SCHOOL A HORSE

BY

E. L. ANDERSON.

Crown 8vo. Price, 2s. 6d.

"It requires the study of only a very few pages of this book to convince the reader that the author thoroughly understands his subject."--*Illustrated Sporting and Dramatic News.*

"Concise, practical directions for riding and training, by which the pupil may become his own master."--*Land and Water.*

"A useful and carefully-written volume."--*Sporting Times.*

"It is sensible and practical."--*Whitehall Review.*

"We cordially commend this book."--*Indian Daily News.*

"The work is a good riding-master's book, with no superfluous words, and with plain, straightforward directions throughout. The chapter on 'The Walk and the Trot' seems to us especially practical and good."--*Farmer.*

"Goes straight to the core of the subject, and is throughout replete with sound sense."--*Home News.*

"Cannot fail to be of service to the young equestrian, while it contains many hints that may be advantageously borne in mind by experienced riders."--*Scotsman.*

"Mr. Anderson gives good practical advice, and we commend the work to the attention of our readers."--*Live Stock Journal.*

London: W. H. ALLEN & CO., 13 Waterloo Place.

THE ILLUSTRATED HORSE DOCTOR

Being an Accurate and Detailed Account, accompanied by more than 400 Pictorial Representations, characteristic of the various Diseases to which the Equine Race are subjected; together with the latest Mode of Treatment, and all the requisite Prescriptions written in Plain English.

By EDWARD MAYHEW, M.R.C.V.S.

8vo., 18*s.* 6*d.*

CONTENTS.--The Brain and Nervous System.--The Eyes.--The Mouth.--The Nostrils.--The Throat.--The Chest and its contents.-- The Stomach, Liver, &c.--The Abdomen.--The Urinary Organs.--The Skin.--Specific Diseases.--Limbs.--The Feet.--Injuries.--Operations.

"The book contains nearly 600 pages of valuable matter, which reflects great credit on its author, and, owing to its practical details, the result of deep scientific research, deserves a place in the library of medical, veterinary, and non-professional readers."--*Field.*

"The book furnishes at once the bane and the antidote, as the drawings show the horse not only suffering from every kind of disease, but in the different stages of it, while the alphabetical summary at the end gives the cause, symptoms and treatment of each."--*Illustrated London News.*

ILLUSTRATED HORSE MANAGEMENT.

Containing Descriptive Remarks upon Anatomy, Medicine, Shoeing, Teeth, Food, Vices, Stables; likewise a plain account of the situation, nature, and value of the various points; together with comments on grooms, dealers, breeders, breakers, and trainers. Embellished with more than 400 engravings from original designs made expressly for this work.

By E. MAYHEW.

A New Edition, Revised and Improved, 8*vo.*, 12*s.*,

By J. I. LUPTON, M.R.C.V.S.

CONTENTS:--The body of the horse anatomically considered. *Physic.* --The mode of administering it, and minor operations. *Shoeing.*-- Its origin, its uses, and its varieties. *The Teeth.*--Their natural growth, and the abuses to which they are liable. *Food.*--The fittest time for feeding, and the kind of food which the horse naturally consumes. The evils which are occasioned by modern stables. The faults inseparable from stables. The so-called "incapacitating vices," which are the results of injury or of disease. Stables as they should be. *Grooms.*--Their prejudices, their injuries, and their duties. *Points.*--Their relative importance, and where to look for their development. *Breeding.*--Its inconsistencies and its disappointments. *Breaking and Training.*--Their errors and their results.

LONDON: W. H. ALLEN & CO., 13 WATERLOO PLACE.

SELECTION FROM

W. H. Allen & Co.'s Catalogue.

SKETCHES FROM NIPAL. Historical and Descriptive, with Anecdotes of Court Life and Wild Sports of the country in the Time of Maharaja Jang Bahadur, G.C.B. With Illustrations of Religious Monuments, Architecture, and Scenery, from the Author's own Drawings. By the late HENRY AMBROSE OLDFIELD, M.D., many years Residency Surgeon at Khatmandu, Nipal. 2 vols. 8vo., 36*s.*

"The work is full of facts, intelligently observed and faithfully recorded."--*Saturday Review.*

"We have nothing but unqualified praise for the manner in which Dr. Oldfield's manuscript has been edited and published by his relatives. The sketches have just claims to rank very high amongst the standard works on the Kingdoms of High Asia."--*Spectator.*

RECORDS OF SPORT AND MILITARY LIFE IN WESTERN INDIA. By the late Lieutenant-Colonel G. T. FRASER, formerly of the 1st Bombay Fusiliers, and more recently attached to the Staff of H.M.'s Indian Army. With an Introduction by Colonel G. B. MALLESON, C.S.I. Crown 8vo., 7*s.* 6*d.*

"The style is free from humbug and affectation, and none of the stories are incredible.... Some of the anecdotes about the early life of Outram confirm the opinion of that gallant officer held by his contemporaries."--*Saturday Review.*

"Records his experience in a very simple and unaffected manner, and he has stirring stories to tell."--*Spectator.*

THIRTEEN YEARS AMONG THE WILD BEASTS OF INDIA; THEIR HAUNTS AND HABITS. From Personal Observation; with an account of the Modes of Capturing and Taming Wild Elephants. By G. P. SANDERSON, Officer in Charge of the Government Elephant Keddahs at Mysore. With 21 full-page Illustrations and Three Maps. Second Edition. Fcp. 4to. £1 5s.

LATCHFORD & WILLSON,

11, UPPER ST. MARTIN'S LANE,

LONDON, W.C.,

By Appointment to HER MAJESTY, H.R.H. THE PRINCE OF WALES, &c. &c.

MAKERS

OF ALL KINDS OF

BRIDLE-BITS, STIRRUPS, & SPURS.

ALL MODERN FASHIONS, ARMY REGULATIONS, &c.

THE LORINER: Latchford on Bridle-bits and the Bitting of Horses. Illustrated, 7s.

PRIZE MEDAL, PARIS.

Just Published, Price 2s. 6d.,

A SYSTEM OF SCHOOL TRAINING FOR HORSES.

By E. L. ANDERSON,

AUTHOR OF "HOW TO RIDE AND SCHOOL A HORSE."

"He is well worthy of a hearing."--*Bell's Life.*

"There is no reason why the careful reader should not be able, by the help of this little book, to train as well as ride his horse."--*Land and Water.*

"Each successive stage of the school system is carefully traced, and anyone accustomed to the management of horses will therefore be able to follow and appreciate the value of Mr. Anderson's kindly method of training."--*Daily Chronicle.*

London: W. H. ALLEN & CO., 13 Waterloo Place.

W. CLARK'S Newly-invented PASTE, for Harness, Patent and Enamelled Leathers. This preparation does not wash off, it renders the leather soft, and produces a polish superior to any of its kind in existence.

W. CLARK'S PLATE POWDER, for Cleansing and Restoring Plate, Brass, and Metals of every description.

W. CLARK'S SADDLE PASTE, for Softening, Preserving, and Beautifying Saddles, Bridles, and every description of Brown Leather, &c.

W. CLARK'S METROPOLITAN POLISH. This article is used for Ladies' and Gentlemen's Patent, Enamel, Bronze Glace, Morocco, Kid Boots and Shoes, producing a superior polish.

W. CLARK'S PATENT KID REVIVER, for cleaning Black Kid Boots and Shoes, making them equal to new, also for reviving all kinds of Black, Blue, and Dark Silks, removes grease spots.

W. CLARK'S NE PLUS ULTRA RAVEN JET FRENCH VARNISH, for Ladies' and Gentlemen's Evening Dress and ordinary Walking Boots and Shoes, producing a most brilliant polish, warranted not to crack or soil the finest Cambric.

W. CLARK'S BRASS PASTE produces a fine polish upon Brass, Copper, Tin, Pewter, Britannia Metal, Coach Glasses, and Windows.

W. CLARK'S WATERPROOF POUCH PASTE, for Pouches, Belts, Straps, Knapsacks, Canteen Coverings, Boots, Leggings &c.

W. CLARK'S EMBROCATION FOR HORSES AND CATTLE, gives immediate relief in all cases of Lameness, Sore Throat, Influenza, and Rheumatism.

W. CLARK'S

PATENT HORSE CLIPPERS.

[Illustration: No. 1.]

Has been before the Public for 12 years, giving the greatest satisfaction, the cheapest and best in the market.

[Illustration: No. 2]

A one-handed Machine for Heads, Ears, Necks, Quarters, Stomachs, Stifle, and all difficult parts; also extensively used in cutting the human hair in hot climates, where it is required to be cut close.

SADDLERY, HARNESS, HORSE CLOTHING &c.

Saddlers by Appointment.

URCH & CO.,

(ESTABLISHED 1835,)

84, LONG ACRE, LONDON, W.C.

MANUFACTURERS OF EVERY DESCRIPTION OF SADDLERY, HARNESS, &c.

WHOLESALE AND RETAIL.

A LARGE ASSORTMENT ALWAYS KEPT IN STOCK.

URCH and CO.'S PATENT DOUBLE SPRING BAR for Releasing the Stirrup Leather when thrown, can be seen at the above establishment "in working order."

By Appointment to H.M. THE QUEEN OF ENGLAND.

By Appointment to H.M. THE QUEEN OF DENMARK.

REDFERN,

LADIES' TAILORS,

By Special Appointments

To H.R.H. THE PRINCESS OF WALES and H.I.H. THE EMPRESS OF RUSSIA,

26, CONDUIT STREET,

Bond Street, London, W.

SPECIALITIES--

RIDING HABITS,

From specially prepared Melton Cloths, &c.

JOHN REDFERN and SONS would particularly draw the attention of Ladies to their Improvements in the cut of Riding Habit Skirts, on the proper set of which depends the whole effect of the Habit. These improvements, while maintaining a tight, well-fitting appearance, give perfect comfort and safety to the rider.

DRIVING COATS,

From Waterproofed Box-Cloths, Faced Cloths, Tweeds, &c.

These, together with J. R. and Son's Improved Newmarket Coats, will be found most useful for driving to meet and for constant wear.

Branch Businesses at Cowes, Isle of Wight, and 242, Rue de Rivoli (Place de la Concorde), Paris.

"The most noted Firm of Ladies' Tailors in the world, and, be it said, the most original."--Extract from *Court Journal.*

By Appointment to H.M. THE QUEEN OF ENGLAND.

By Appointment to H.M. THE QUEEN OF DENMARK.

REDFERN,

LADIES' TAILORS,

By Special Appointments

TO H.R.H. THE PRINCESS OF WALES AND H.I.H. THE EMPRESS OF RUSSIA,

26, CONDUIT STREET,

BOND STREET, LONDON, W.

SPECIALITY--

YACHTING & TRAVELLING GOWNS.

*** From original Colourings in Cloth and Serge, &c.

The Firm personally superintend every order, and a perfect fit is guaranteed.

N.B.--On the occasion of the visit to England of H.S.H. the Princess Helena of Waldeck, in March 1882, John Redfern and Sons had the honour of making for Her Serene Highness.

On the visit of H.I.M. the Empress Eugenie, accompanied by the late Napoleon III., J. R. and Sons had a similar honour.

On the visit of H.I.H. the Crown Princess of Germany, J. R. and Sons had the honour of making for Her Imperial Highness and all the Princesses.

On the visit to the Queen of T.R.H. the Princesses of Hesse Darmstadt, J. R. and Sons had the honour of making for their Royal Highnesses.

On the visit to Her Majesty of the Daughters of H.R.H. the late Princess Alice, J. R. and Sons had a similar honour.

Branch Businesses at Cowes, Isle of Wight, and 242, Rue de Rivoli (Place de la Concorde), Paris.

"The most noted Firm of Ladies' Tailors in the world, and, be it said, the most original."--Extract from *Court Journal*.

LADIES' RIDING BOOTS.

ESTABLISHED 1839.

N. THIERRY,

ESTABLISHED 1839.

LADIES' AND GENTLEMEN'S

BOOT & SHOE MANUFACTURER,

LONDON, {70 QUADRANT, REGENT STREET, W., {AND 48, GRESHAM STREET, E.C.

MANCHESTER, 2, St. Ann's Sq.; LIVERPOOL, 5, Bold St.

Complete Illustrated Price Lists Post Free.

[Illustration: LADIES' RIDING BOOT, 50s., all Patent or with Morocco Legs.]

NO INFERIOR ARTICLES KEPT. ALL GOODS WARRANTED AND MARKED IN PLAIN FIGURES.

THE LARGEST STOCK OF BEST QUALITY GOODS IN ENGLAND ALWAYS READY. 26,000 PAIRS TO CHOOSE FROM.

[Illustration: LADIES' NEWMARKET RIDING BOOT, Cloth legs, 50s.]

NOTE.--*To order, 2s. per pair extra for fitting and keeping special lasts.*

LADIES' SPURS, Silver Plate, Strap, & Buckle complete, 9s, 6d.

PRICE LIST of a few Leading Articles, Ladies' Department:--

BOOTS.

Button or Lace 17s. 0d. Do. do. Hessians, from 19s. 6d. Do. do. Cork Clumps 24s. 0d. Do. High Glacé Louis XV. Heels 27s. 29s.

SHOES.

Oxford Tie, Morocco 14s. 0d. Do. do. Glacé 16s. 0d. Do. Richelieu, Louis XV. Heels 23s. 0d. Patent Court Heels and

Bows 8s. 6d. Glacé Kid, Embroidered. 11s. 6d.

A GREAT VARIETY of very Fashionable Ladies' Dress Shoes in Glace Kid or Satin (various Colours), Embroidered Jet, Gold, Steel, or Bijou.

A LARGE ASSORTMENT OF CHILDREN'S BOOTS AND SHOES,

AND EVERY VARIETY OF GENTS' RIDING, WALKING, & DRESS BOOTS & SHOES.

Goods sent on approval on receipt of satisfactory references (a London tradesman preferred), or cheque for the amount. An old boot or shoe should be sent as a guide for size, paper patterns and other measurements being of little use. Goods that do not suit will be exchanged or the money returned.

FIVE PER CENT. DISCOUNT FOR CASH.

PLEASE NOTE--70, REGENT STREET QUADRANT, as there is another house of the same Surname in the street.

Archive/American Libraries.)

Updated editions will replace the previous one--the old editions will be renamed.

Creating the works from public domain print editions means that no one owns a United States copyright in these works, so the Foundation (and you!) can copy and distribute it in the United States without permission and without paying copyright royalties. Special rules, set forth in the General Terms of Use part of this license, apply to copying and distributing Project Gutenberg-tm electronic works to protect the PROJECT GUTENBERG-tm concept and trademark. Project Gutenberg is a registered trademark, and may not be used if you charge for the eBooks, unless you receive specific permission. If you do not charge anything for copies of this eBook, complying with the rules is very easy. You may use this eBook for nearly any purpose such as creation of derivative works, reports, performances and research. They may be modified and printed and given away--you may do practically ANYTHING with public domain eBooks. Redistribution is subject to the trademark license, especially commercial redistribution.

*** START: FULL LICENSE ***

THE FULL PROJECT GUTENBERG LICENSE PLEASE READ THIS BEFORE YOU DISTRIBUTE OR USE THIS WORK

To protect the Project Gutenberg-tm mission of promoting the free distribution of electronic works, by using or distributing this work (or any other work associated in any way with the phrase "Project Gutenberg"), you agree to comply with all the terms of the Full Project Gutenberg-tm License available with this file or online at www.gutenberg.org/license.

Section 1. General Terms of Use and Redistributing Project Gutenberg-tm electronic works

1.A. By reading or using any part of this Project Gutenberg-tm electronic work, you indicate that you have read, understand, agree to and accept all the terms of this license and intellectual property (trademark/copyright) agreement. If you do not agree to abide by all the terms of this agreement, you must cease using and return or destroy all copies of Project Gutenberg-tm electronic works in your possession. If you paid a fee for obtaining a copy of or access to a Project Gutenberg-tm electronic work and you do not agree to be bound by the terms of this agreement, you may obtain a refund from the person or entity to whom you paid the fee as set forth in paragraph 1.E.8.

1.B. "Project Gutenberg" is a registered trademark. It may only be used on or associated in any way with an electronic work by people who agree to be bound by the terms of this agreement. There are a few things that you can do with most Project Gutenberg-tm electronic works even without complying with the full terms of this agreement. See paragraph 1.C below. There are a lot of things you can do with Project Gutenberg-tm electronic works if you follow the terms of this agreement and help preserve free future access to Project Gutenberg-tm electronic works. See paragraph 1.E below.

1.C. The Project Gutenberg Literary Archive Foundation ("the Foundation" or PGLAF), owns a compilation copyright in the collection of Project Gutenberg-tm electronic works. Nearly all the individual works in the collection are in the public domain in the United States. If an individual work is in the public domain in the United States and you are located in the United States, we do not claim a right to prevent you from copying, distributing, performing, displaying or creating derivative works based on the work as long as all references to Project Gutenberg are removed. Of course, we hope that you will support the Project

Gutenberg-tm mission of promoting free access to electronic works by freely sharing Project Gutenberg-tm works in compliance with the terms of this agreement for keeping the Project Gutenberg-tm name associated with the work. You can easily comply with the terms of this agreement by keeping this work in the same format with its attached full Project Gutenberg-tm License when you share it without charge with others.

1.D. The copyright laws of the place where you are located also govern what you can do with this work. Copyright laws in most countries are in a constant state of change. If you are outside the United States, check the laws of your country in addition to the terms of this agreement before downloading, copying, displaying, performing, distributing or creating derivative works based on this work or any other Project Gutenberg-tm work. The Foundation makes no representations concerning the copyright status of any work in any country outside the United States.

1.E. Unless you have removed all references to Project Gutenberg:

1.E.1. The following sentence, with active links to, or other immediate access to, the full Project Gutenberg-tm License must appear prominently whenever any copy of a Project Gutenberg-tm work (any work on which the phrase "Project Gutenberg" appears, or with which the phrase "Project Gutenberg" is associated) is accessed, displayed, performed, viewed, copied or distributed:

This eBook is for the use of anyone anywhere at no cost and with almost no restrictions whatsoever. You may copy it, give it away or re-use it under the terms of the Project Gutenberg License included with this eBook or online at www.gutenberg.org

1.E.2. If an individual Project Gutenberg-tm electronic work is derived from the public domain (does not contain a notice indicating that it is posted with permission of the copyright holder), the work can be copied and distributed to anyone in the United States without paying any fees or charges. If you are redistributing or providing access to a work with the phrase "Project Gutenberg" associated with or appearing on the work, you must comply either with the requirements of paragraphs 1.E.1 through 1.E.7 or obtain permission for the use of the work and the Project Gutenberg-tm trademark as set forth in paragraphs 1.E.8 or 1.E.9.

1.E.3. If an individual Project Gutenberg-tm electronic work is posted with the permission of the copyright holder, your use and distribution must comply with both paragraphs 1.E.1 through 1.E.7 and any additional terms imposed by the copyright holder. Additional terms will be linked to the Project Gutenberg-tm License for all works posted with the permission of the copyright holder found at the beginning of this work.

1.E.4. Do not unlink or detach or remove the full Project Gutenberg-tm License terms from this work, or any files containing a part of this work or any other work associated with Project Gutenberg-tm.

1.E.5. Do not copy, display, perform, distribute or redistribute this electronic work, or any part of this electronic work, without prominently displaying the sentence set forth in paragraph 1.E.1 with active links or immediate access to the full terms of the Project Gutenberg-tm License.

1.E.6. You may convert to and distribute this work in any binary, compressed, marked up, nonproprietary or proprietary form, including any word processing or hypertext form. However, if you provide access to or distribute copies of a Project Gutenberg-tm work in a format other than "Plain Vanilla ASCII" or other format used in the official version posted on the official Project Gutenberg-tm web site (www.gutenberg.org), you must, at no additional cost, fee or expense to the user, provide a copy, a means of exporting a copy, or a means of obtaining a copy upon request, of the work in its original "Plain Vanilla ASCII" or other form. Any alternate format must include the full Project Gutenberg-tm License as specified in paragraph 1.E.1.

1.E.7. Do not charge a fee for access to, viewing, displaying, performing, copying or distributing any Project Gutenberg-tm works unless you comply with paragraph 1.E.8 or 1.E.9.

1.E.8. You may charge a reasonable fee for copies of or providing access to or distributing Project Gutenberg-tm electronic works provided that

- You pay a royalty fee of 20% of the gross profits you derive from the use of Project Gutenberg-tm works calculated using the method you already use to calculate your applicable taxes. The fee is owed to the owner of the Project Gutenberg-tm trademark, but he has agreed to donate royalties under this paragraph to the Project Gutenberg Literary Archive Foundation. Royalty payments must be paid within 60 days following each date on which you prepare (or are legally required to prepare) your periodic tax returns. Royalty payments should be clearly marked as such and sent to the Project Gutenberg Literary Archive Foundation at the address specified in Section 4, "Information about donations to the Project Gutenberg Literary Archive Foundation."

- You provide a full refund of any money paid by a user who notifies you in writing (or by e-mail) within 30 days of receipt that s/he does not agree to the terms of the full Project Gutenberg-tm License. You must require such a user to return or destroy all copies of the works possessed in a physical medium and discontinue all use of and all access to other copies of Project

Gutenberg-tm works.

- You provide, in accordance with paragraph 1.F.3, a full refund of any money paid for a work or a replacement copy, if a defect in the electronic work is discovered and reported to you within 90 days of receipt of the work.

- You comply with all other terms of this agreement for free distribution of Project Gutenberg-tm works.

1.E.9. If you wish to charge a fee or distribute a Project Gutenberg-tm electronic work or group of works on different terms than are set forth in this agreement, you must obtain permission in writing from both the Project Gutenberg Literary Archive Foundation and Michael Hart, the owner of the Project Gutenberg-tm trademark. Contact the Foundation as set forth in Section 3 below.

1.F.

1.F.1. Project Gutenberg volunteers and employees expend considerable effort to identify, do copyright research on, transcribe and proofread public domain works in creating the Project Gutenberg-tm collection. Despite these efforts, Project Gutenberg-tm electronic works, and the medium on which they may be stored, may contain "Defects," such as, but not limited to, incomplete, inaccurate or corrupt data, transcription errors, a copyright or other intellectual property infringement, a defective or damaged disk or other medium, a computer virus, or computer codes that damage or cannot be read by your equipment.

1.F.2. LIMITED WARRANTY, DISCLAIMER OF DAMAGES - Except for the "Right of Replacement or Refund" described in paragraph 1.F.3, the Project Gutenberg Literary Archive Foundation, the owner of the Project Gutenberg-tm trademark, and any other party distributing a Project Gutenberg-tm electronic work under this agreement, disclaim all liability to you for damages, costs and expenses, including legal fees. YOU AGREE THAT YOU HAVE NO REMEDIES FOR NEGLIGENCE, STRICT LIABILITY, BREACH OF WARRANTY OR BREACH OF CONTRACT EXCEPT THOSE PROVIDED IN PARAGRAPH 1.F.3. YOU AGREE THAT THE FOUNDATION, THE TRADEMARK OWNER, AND ANY DISTRIBUTOR UNDER THIS AGREEMENT WILL NOT BE LIABLE TO YOU FOR ACTUAL, DIRECT, INDIRECT, CONSEQUENTIAL, PUNITIVE OR INCIDENTAL DAMAGES EVEN IF YOU GIVE NOTICE OF THE POSSIBILITY OF SUCH DAMAGE.

1.F.3. LIMITED RIGHT OF REPLACEMENT OR REFUND - If you discover a defect in this electronic work within 90 days of receiving it, you can receive a refund of the money (if any) you paid for it by sending a written explanation to the person you received the work from. If you received the work on a physical medium, you must return the medium with your written explanation. The person or entity that provided you with the defective work may elect to provide a replacement copy in lieu of a refund. If you received the work electronically, the person or entity providing it to you may choose to give you a second opportunity to receive the work electronically in lieu of a refund. If the second copy is also defective, you may demand a refund in writing without further opportunities to fix the problem.

1.F.4. Except for the limited right of replacement or refund set forth in paragraph 1.F.3, this work is provided to you 'AS-IS', WITH NO OTHER WARRANTIES OF ANY KIND, EXPRESS OR IMPLIED, INCLUDING BUT NOT LIMITED TO WARRANTIES OF MERCHANTABILITY OR FITNESS FOR ANY PURPOSE.

1.F.5. Some states do not allow disclaimers of certain implied warranties or the exclusion or limitation of certain types of damages. If any disclaimer or limitation set forth in this agreement violates the law of the state applicable to this agreement, the agreement shall be interpreted to make the maximum disclaimer or limitation permitted by the applicable state law. The invalidity or unenforceability of any provision of this agreement shall not void the remaining provisions.

1.F.6. **INDEMNITY**

- You agree to indemnify and hold the Foundation, the trademark owner, any agent or employee of the Foundation, anyone providing copies of Project Gutenberg-tm electronic works in accordance with this agreement, and any volunteers associated with the production, promotion and distribution of Project Gutenberg-tm electronic works, harmless from all liability, costs and expenses, including legal fees, that arise directly or indirectly from any of the following which you do or cause to occur: (a) distribution of this or any Project Gutenberg-tm work, (b) alteration, modification, or additions or deletions to any Project Gutenberg-tm work, and (c) any Defect you cause.

Section 2. Information about the Mission of Project Gutenberg-tm

Project Gutenberg-tm is synonymous with the free distribution of electronic works in formats readable by the widest variety of computers including obsolete, old, middle-aged and new computers. It exists because of the efforts of hundreds of volunteers and donations from people in all walks of life.

Volunteers and financial support to provide volunteers with the assistance they need are critical to reaching Project Gutenberg-tm's goals and ensuring that the Project Gutenberg-tm collection will remain freely available for generations to come. In 2001, the Project Gutenberg Literary Archive Foundation was created to provide a secure and permanent future for Project Gutenberg-tm and future generations. To learn more about the Project Gutenberg Literary Archive Foundation and how your efforts and donations can help, see Sections 3 and 4 and the Foundation information page at www.gutenberg.org

Section 3. Information about the Project Gutenberg Literary Archive Foundation

The Project Gutenberg Literary Archive Foundation is a non profit 501(c)(3) educational corporation organized under the laws of the state of Mississippi and granted tax exempt status by the Internal Revenue Service. The Foundation's EIN or federal tax identification number is 64-6221541. Contributions to the Project Gutenberg Literary Archive Foundation are tax deductible to the full extent permitted by U.S. federal laws and your state's laws.

The Foundation's principal office is located at 4557 Melan Dr. S. Fairbanks, AK, 99712., but its volunteers and employees are scattered throughout numerous locations. Its business office is located at 809 North 1500 West, Salt Lake City, UT 84116, (801) 596-1887. Email contact links and up to date contact information can be found at the Foundation's web site and official page at www.gutenberg.org/contact

For additional contact information: Dr. Gregory B. Newby Chief Executive and Director gbnewby@pglaf.org

Section 4. Information about Donations to the Project Gutenberg Literary Archive Foundation

Project Gutenberg-tm depends upon and cannot survive without wide spread public support and donations to carry out its mission of increasing the number of public domain and licensed works that can be freely distributed in machine readable form accessible by the widest array of equipment including outdated equipment. Many small donations ($1 to $5,000) are particularly important to maintaining tax exempt status with the IRS.

The Foundation is committed to complying with the laws regulating charities and charitable donations in all 50 states of the United States. Compliance requirements are not uniform and it takes a considerable effort, much paperwork and many fees to meet and keep up with these requirements. We do not solicit donations in locations where we have not received written confirmation of compliance. To SEND DONATIONS or determine the status of compliance for any particular state visit www.gutenberg.org/donate

While we cannot and do not solicit contributions from states where we have not met the solicitation requirements, we know of no prohibition against accepting unsolicited donations from donors in such states who approach us with offers to donate.

International donations are gratefully accepted, but we cannot make any statements concerning tax treatment of donations received from outside the United States. U.S. laws alone swamp our small staff.

Please check the Project Gutenberg Web pages for current donation methods and addresses. Donations are accepted in a number of other ways including checks, online payments and credit card donations. To donate, please visit: www.gutenberg.org/donate

Section 5. General Information About Project Gutenberg-tm electronic works.

Professor Michael S. Hart was the originator of the Project Gutenberg-tm concept of a library of electronic works that could be freely shared with anyone. For forty years, he produced and distributed Project Gutenberg-tm eBooks with only a loose network of volunteer support.

Ladies on Horseback, by Nannie Lambert